FOLLOW THE FEELING

A Roadmap to Emotional Freedom

Lisa West

Spiralling-In Publications

The author of this book is not a physician and the ideas, procedures and suggestions in this book are not intended as a substitute for the medical advice of a trained health professional. All matters regarding your health require medical supervision. Consult your physician or counselor before adopting the suggestions in this book, as well as about any condition that may require diagnosis or medical intervention. The author and publisher disclaim any liability arising directly or indirectly from the use of this book.

Spiralling-In Publications
PO Box 7264
Oxnard, CA 93031

Cover Design Copyright @ 2019 by Kristen Smith
Cover Art by Tom Hardcastle
Book Design by Catherine Baker
Author Photo by Rebecca Gaal

Publisher's Cataloging-in-Publication data

Names: West, Lisa C., author.
Titles: Follow the feeling : a roadmap to emotional freedom / Lisa West.
Description: Includes bibliographical references. |
Oxnard, CA: Spiralling-In Publications, 2019.
Identifiers: LCCN 2018914402 | ISBN 978-1-7329166-0-9 (pbk.) |
978-1-7329166-1-6 (ebook)
Subjects: LCSH Meditation. | Stress (Psychology) | Stress management.
| Well-being. | BISAC BODY, MIND & SPIRIT / Mindfulness &
Meditation
Classification: LCC BL627 .W44 2019 | DDC 158.1/2--dc23

To download the included audio meditations, visit
LisaWestWellness.com/book-audio

Enter this code

916609

To purchase the entire audio meditation set, visit

LisaWestWellness.com/follow-the-feeling-album

Contents

* Meditations marked with 🎧 will be available to download and listen to at LisaWestWellness.com/book-audio.

Foreword

What a wonderful book! Such a clear, profound message. Follow the feeling . . . of course! Where else could it lead but to the Source of all? And, therefore, to the realization that you and I are quite literally the expressions of that source. That is the healing message here.

This small book is replete with grounded, practical advice about how to follow whatever you are feeling from grief to joy. None of the exercises are particularly difficult. Many of the techniques involve breathing, something we all do every day. All the techniques can help you follow the feeling connected to whatever you are experiencing into the truth/essence of who and what you are. You will garner a clearer understanding about what may have been bothering you, and how to remedy it.

The reluctance many of us experience with regard to doing this revolves around the fear that following an unpleasant feeling could actually be devastating. We could get increasingly enmeshed in the problem, more than we already are. We may not be able to find our way out again. It may even make things worse. Allowing yourself to experience more joy than you are accustomed to could turn you into some sort of addict and get you into trouble. Sure, you have to risk the chance. It doesn't always make intuitive sense to "feel the grief" or even "follow your bliss." Who knows what might happen? There is often tremendous resistance experienced at this point.

The lure, however, lies in the rumor that there is something marvelous awaiting you in the now, on the other side of whatever the current feeling happens to be. Add to that the fact that more often than not, whatever you are experiencing now is being experienced as a problem or is painful and enough is enough. Your deepest knowing declares, "I deserve more satisfaction than I am currently experiencing."

The happy discovery is that joy and sanity are the underlying, all-embracing, surround-sound feeling-tones of conscious being—your being. This is no small insight and (especially if it's true) it's the worthy prize of such a risk. As Lisa points out, "Feelings never killed anyone." This assurance can promote the courage necessary to feel into the scary parts with less fear, and enjoy the pleasurable parts more fully, with less reluctance or reservation.

The growing realization is that we are bigger than whatever we are experiencing. Therefore, we are fundamentally safe, and we can experience that as fact. Following the feeling culminates in wisdom, epitomized as the willingness to follow your heart. Following your heart will not only elicit a more harmonious, personally fulfilling experience, but will translate into a kinder and better world.

— ERICH SCHIFFMANN has gained international recognition for his unique approach to yoga. He studied and taught yoga at the Krishnamurti School in England in the 1970s before studying in India with Iyengar and returning to Southern California. He is the author of the seminal work *YOGA: The Spirit and Practice of Moving into Stillness*.

Preface

Swimming in the Deep End: My Story

I have a long history of repressing my feelings. I was an expert at "being happy." I saw the best in everyone. I immediately conjured up excuses and rationale for bad behavior and went straight to forgiveness while skipping right over the hurt and the pain, the grief, the fear and the anger. All the while I didn't realize that fear was what was keeping me in this "happy" place. If I made a convincing enough argument that all was well, then I didn't have to look at those scary places that had been bubbling within for my entire life (and likely longer).

Being liked and being a "good girl" has its obvious advantages. If you please everyone around you, you gain love and acceptance. You don't cause any waves that might facilitate "ugly" emotions like fear, guilt, shame, rejection, or the really scary ones like anger, envy, and hatred. It works pretty well to "be good" as a child. You get high marks in school and you're rewarded. You do what your parents say, and they are pleased. All of those ugly ways you acted as a toddler get stuffed inside as "undesirables," and you learn how to function and thrive in the world around you. You create new parts of your personality.

The façade begins to crack, however, when those pesky hormones come into play during puberty. Though I still maintained decent grades and was a well-behaved kid, my anger and resentment and even hatred came out with a vengeance as I tried to individuate from my parents. They got raging screams and tantrums as my repressed inner-self emerged. I tried desperately to keep being good through it all, but this force was stronger than the personality I had cultivated. It was often easier to hate my parents and withdraw into the comfort of my friends who, in my eyes, were my saviors, the only ones who understood how unfair and awful my parents were.

Let me qualify what I mean by awful. I was raised by amazingly loving parents in the 1970s when child-rearing techniques were different than they are today. People started having children when they were young. The advent of formula feeding and Dr. Spock child-rearing methods were all the rage, and the experts were saying it was best to let your child individuate right away, as a newborn. Studies since have shown that initial bonding and establishing safety and security are an essential part of child development, and that breastfeeding, skin-to-skin contact and immediate response to a newborn's cries help to establish that sense of security.

Ideas about discipline were also quite different than they are now. Parents were taught that they needed to show their children right from wrong (not such a bad idea), but they were also taught that physical and emotional/psychological punishment were effective ways to communicate this concept. They were raised to equate discipline with control and domination. The Pavlovian method of reward and punishment had proved effective at behavior modification, which on the surface was the primary objective.

There are many ideas about child-rearing, and still much debate about what is best for healthy child development. The most recent data points to leading by example as the most effective way to teach children how to appropriately function in the world. My intention is not to say what is right or wrong. I don't think there are black and white answers to questions or a right or wrong way to do just about anything. Instead, I want to show that these methods and beliefs were norms when I was growing up. Parents of that era were routinely told by experts (and learned from their own upbringing) to ignore their instincts (tending to a crying baby) for the good of the child. They were shown that physical discipline would guarantee well-adjusted, functional human beings. They were doing the best they could with the information available to them.

For me, this point is important. My parents loved me very much. They wanted the best for me. They are good, loving people. They weren't addicts or intentionally abusive. They weren't rageaholics or sociopaths. They were two people, who, as I did, learned how to "be good" and feel guilt or shame for having unapproved emotions.

Therefore in my world and in my mind, I had no logical reason to be resentful, angry, hateful, fearful, grief stricken or sad. When those "bad" thoughts or feelings surfaced, with them came shame and insecurity leading to an eventual loss of trust in my own instincts and emotions.

Instead of forging a healthy and accepting relationship with my "negative" feelings, I stuffed them down and regarded those aspects of myself as bad, which made me a bad person for having them. Just as my feelings began to leak out as a teenager, I could see it happen to my parents from time to time. There were moments of explosion and frustration and rage, and moments of teasing and passive-aggressive behavior, condescension, shame and guilt tactics. Because I was acting out in the same ways, I recognized these behaviors as attempts to truly be seen and heard.

I was born an exceptionally sensitive soul into a sensitive body (my greatest gift), so my emotions were heightened, requiring me to build a suit of armor to shield myself from so many sensations. I became a master at the art of repression and internalization of "negative feelings." And the terror that held it all together was massive.

As these feelings began to surface in my teenage years and into my early twenties, I burned off a lot of the energy through competitive swimming. What a perfect venue for a young girl who was learning to hate these big feelings and herself. I could spend hours alone, letting the energy move out through physical means—a strategy I highly recommend. Whatever was left could be funneled into self-punishment and criticism for not swimming perfectly or getting a personal-best time—

a strategy I do not recommend. There was a lot of joy in swimming, too. It enabled me to express myself physically and be part of a community of wonderful people, yet it provided the spacious joy of being by myself, head underwater, meditating on my own breath. If I had to take a guess, swimming probably saved my so-called teenage life. In giving me a healthy outlet, it let me delay my journey into my deep, dark feelings.

I was never a great swimmer, but I was good. I was able to win a modest scholarship to a Division One college to pursue a career I was so clearly called to that I didn't even have to deliberate: physical therapy. I was lucky to have known from childhood that I would choose a career in the medical field. I had called it "doctor" until I had an injury as a high school swimmer and went to my first physical therapist. The level of time and personal connection involved with physical therapy resonated immediately and I knew I'd found the field for me.

My college years were fun. I loved my swim team, I loved my coursework, I loved my job as a librarian, and I especially loved the social life that college offered along with the freedom to shed a little of the good girl façade through the abundant availability of alcohol and drugs. (I was still a good girl, though, so only modestly excessive.)

The summer of my junior year of college (the most challenging year) a couple of my good friends went through very dark experiences, including suicide attempts and heroin use. I don't know if it was the stress and overwhelm of these situations or my guilt about the strong negative feelings I was experiencing despite a life that was "so good by comparison," or the 10 pounds of beer and pizza weight I had gained. Maybe it was the self-hatred that was manifesting (an unfortunate side effect of denying that you have unsavory feelings). After years of introspection, I still don't know for sure what triggered it, but that summer I decided to stop eating.

I have always been very thin. When I was 16, my physician told my parents I should have a milkshake daily to help me gain weight. I was teased about it when I was younger and never felt comfortable in my skin. I do know that I never felt fat until I noticed the slight weight gain in college. This seems important to share because it highlights that "being skinny" wasn't the primary motivation for me to stop eating. I suspect it rarely is the main reason people starve themselves. It likely has more to do with self-loathing, wanting to disappear, wanting to repress feelings and a need to hold it all together. Control? Yes. But to me, it was less about external situations and more about the feelings I couldn't tolerate. I can't imagine that it's clear to anyone who is anorexic that they are starving themselves to avoid feeling. I also wanted to starve myself to remove the vitality of who I was. Instead of being able to see my negative emotions as a valid part of myself, I began to define myself by them. I had no right to feel these strong emotions, and I hated myself for having them. I certainly didn't have awareness around my motivations until I was much older and started to have an emotional and sensory relationship with my belly and my sweet, tender heart.

At the time I decided to stop eating, I didn't know why. I was just compelled to do so. Once I was aware of the power that resulted from gaining control of that part of my life and how well I could conceal it from others, it became a game, and then an addiction. Something snapped in my brain that forced me to keep it up. I had put on the energetic corset of a queen and could rule the world with my secret and my mastery.

I returned to school that fall to find out that I had lost my swimming scholarship. I remember the pitying look in my coach's eyes when he delivered the news. I remember swallowing my hurt and my shock and how I immediately began making excuses for him—a habit I would continue for years. There were much faster young swimmers coming in and I hadn't had a personal best in over a year. I was going to be missing for the second half of the season because of my clinical rotations for PT school. What I swallowed in that moment was the truth: I lost my scholarship because I had dropped to 88 pounds.

My secret wasn't a secret anymore, but I continued to keep up the belief that it was. I started smoking cigarettes and drinking coffee.

(Black, because I didn't want the calories from the cream or sugar.) I ate just enough to fake it for my family and friends. I dressed in the oversized baby doll dresses and flannels that were favored during the early '90s and dated a man who was obsessed with unhealthily thin girls. My physique was just what he liked and helped to confirm that I was ruling life in my anorexic state.

One day, when I was back in my hometown for my final clinical rotation, my dad pulled me aside and said, "Lisa, I think you are getting too skinny." Instantly something within me changed. Ever the people-pleaser, especially where dad was concerned, I walked upstairs and faced myself in the mirror. I no longer saw the distorted image I'd become accustomed to. I saw an emaciated shell of the thin but athletic person I used to be. I was wearing my twelve-year-old sister's skirt at the time. I realized this wasn't normal. Something clicked inside my brain, and I knew I had to start forcing myself to eat again. As quickly as it had begun, the anorexic phase of my life was over—at least in relation to food.

I began a long process of learning to dive beneath the shell I had created, where I explored the wondrous and rich world of my feelings. I began to discover the expressions of power, strength and authentic expression that existed beneath the façade I had presented to the world. It took a long time to convince myself that it was safe to have such strong emotions, but eventually I began to appreciate and value all of them, even the "unsavory" ones.

I eased into it with yoga when I was 20, which was my introduction to the sensations inside my body. Later, I was exposed to other techniques that gave me tools for self-navigation: Reiki, craniosacral therapy, visceral mobilization and, most transformational of all, John Barnes' Myofascial Release (MFR).

The most profound thing that happened to me, though, was meeting my partner. At 30, I had all kinds of ideas about relationships and what they meant. I had examples all around me of what was good and not so good in a relationship. What I had no idea about was how a relationship could pry you open and poke into your festering wounds to expose what you've kept hidden from yourself and the world. I chose a partner who is unapologetic about his feelings and expressing them clearly, loudly and in the moment. What I had mastered in finesse and polish, he had mastered in raw honesty. I'd found a man with a keen intuitive sense who can smell fraudulence a mile away. And I was the master of disguise and diplomacy.

When two people with such differences meet, there are several options for handling it. Most (probably saner people) run for the hills and find a softer and gentler road into the self. But I'm a competitor who is terribly strong and stubborn. (I was a fabulous anorexic, for example.) So without hesitation, I walked into the fire. And miraculously, so did he. I had met my match in tenacity and follow-through and the willingness to stay through the discomfort. "Discomfort" is sugar coating it. We walked through pain, anguish, heartbreak and despair.

I decided to take my mythical journey into the underworld. It was time to face my demons and the parts of myself I had rejected. It was time to see what I had avoided, and learn the value of those qualities by exploring where they came from and allowing them to be present. It was healthier than trying to plug the small leaks of repressed toxicity, or letting them continue to eat away at me from the inside.

Somehow, a greater part of myself knew that I was prepared for this journey. The healing work that I had decided to offer others was about to give me all of the tools I needed for my own healing. I was about to learn how to come fully into my body and how lovely and rich the experience of being alive on this planet can be. I was about to find the jewels that make me a whole human being. At that time, I was incapable of knowing that those jewels and stored-up bliss were hidden inside the very feelings I was avoiding.

I gradually (and sometimes not so gradually) learned to feel and express myself. As I fine-tuned my skills into noticing the subtleties of my feelings and vibrational expressions, I began to realize that the inner knowing and intuitive, instinctual parts of myself were alive and growing stronger. Because these instincts had been repressed alongside the feelings for so long, it took many years of practice for me to begin trusting this information. And once trusting the emotions became easier, it took even longer for me to start acting on those feelings.

The good news is that this journey gets less extreme and less intense as time goes on, and even when a new layer emerges I've become better at knowing that it's merely an energetic sensation, which helps me to loosen my grip. This usually allows the sensation to pass through quickly into the next expansive layer of light. That was not, however, my experience at the beginning. At first, I resisted the sensations and my mind held onto reasons and stories about why these emotions were there. I was afraid. This made the process more difficult and more painful than it needed to be. It took training and practice to get better at staying present with the feelings and not allow them to carry me off into a downward spiral that could keep me reeling for days.

The more often I trusted what I was feeling and followed that information, the more things started to line up seemingly by magic. I was suddenly shown new options and choices greater than any I could have imagined. Things that I dreamed about became very real possibilities, and I was given a choice between following that option or doing something else equally great. Sometimes the feeling about the open door leads me to walk through it, and sometimes I am guided onto a new path. All I can do is trust in what I feel in every moment. If I listen and follow it, I get to reap the rewards, *even if they are beyond my control.*

I am not a psychologist. I do not claim to have extensive training or knowledge in this realm. I only have the personal experience that being a seasoned myofascial release therapist, bodyworker and yogini have brought me. I have a fascination with the human condition and how the psyche and emotions dance within the physical experience. I have a calling to bring forth as much light into the world as possible. My journey has revealed to me that with every meeting of every new part of myself, with every release of the resistance to being with my deepest feelings, more of my light can shine. I am freer, more open and creative. These are the things that have led me here.

My hope in sharing this story and this book is to help ignite your spark, to give you some practical techniques and insights into navigating those dark areas and finding your way to live in your own light.

Every experience has a gift in it. I am so lucky that I had two parents who loved me deeply. That is such a blessing, and I have never taken it for granted. I am also grateful that I was raised exactly how I was. Through disciplined punishment, I plumbed the depths of victimization, anger and helplessness. I took those feelings and ran with them, continuing to see how far into disempowerment I could venture. My inner punisher was well-developed. That experience has taught me all I know about how it feels to be disempowered and what helps me reclaim my power. Without that experience, being compassionately present for someone who was raped, abused or brought to their knees by pain or illness, would not be possible for me. I still had a tremendous capacity for feeling without having to endure the unthinkable.

Without the old child-rearing practice of letting babies cry it out instead of soothing them, I might not have developed a sensitive nervous system. Without that sensitivity, I might not have been forced to acquire the extensive skills necessary for recalibrating the nervous system toward peace, a skill that I can now share.

Without the experiences of moving around frequently as a kid, I wouldn't have developed my large capacity for adapting to my environment and learning to fully live wherever I am. If I hadn't had four younger siblings, I wouldn't have developed the ability to withdraw my senses amid chaos. I wouldn't have learned how to get along and share with others. I wouldn't have received the gift of navigating those primal feelings of hatred when we fought. Most important, I wouldn't have experienced the joyous laughter, bonding and deep love these oldest and most crucial friends, my siblings, brought to my life.

And, of course, there is the great blessing of the love that my parents modeled for me. They showed me acceptance and kindness. They taught me how to be non-judgmental of people who were different than me. They showed me what commitment and kindness look like through their relationship. Their ability to take things in stride afforded me a thicker skin. They gave me the gift of adventure and travel. They modeled the importance of family. They taught me self-responsibility and how to apologize when needed. They taught me independence and self-reliance. I watched them stay committed and active, bonded and dedicated to each other and to their children.

I am so grateful for every experience I had because it shaped me into who I would become, who I *am*. It laid the groundwork for me. It gave me a reason to investigate my feelings, to know myself more deeply and therefore listen to my feelings and trust them. I have no idea who I would be and what my life's work would be if I had a different set of experiences. Each person has a unique life journey that shapes and allows them the potential for accessing their gifts and their compassionate nature. It's up to the individual to acknowledge the challenges and find a thread of gratitude for each of them.

Introduction

L ife is a wild and exciting journey toward finding ourselves. We are all essentially built from the same stuff, in the same way. Recent discoveries in science and years of contemplative observation show that we respond similarly to many things and that our inner workings are somewhat predictable.

But we are also unique beings. Some of us like adventure, some like quiet. Some people respond to silliness and laughter while others prefer gentleness and bonding. Some people are naturally strong and athletic, some are innately quick-minded and witty, others are calm and rational. We all enjoy some things some of the time. Variety is what keeps us interested in life and interesting to ourselves and others.

My hope for this book is that it offers you many different paths to choose from on the journey into yourself. There will be some people who respond to the quiet and meditative visualizations and some who prefer the active practices. Some people will like music and sound, others prefer beautiful aromas or nature to bring them closer to truth. Some days you will need something easy to do and other days you may want a challenge. Of course, there are those who find they get their best gains from daily repetition and routine.

I urge you to experiment! Try a variety of techniques and suggestions then go back to the ones that feel the most effective. Expect that as you change and grow and as you experience strong days and tired days, you may prefer practices that you hadn't previously resonated with. At times you will even rediscover old gems that used to resonate, but were temporarily forgotten as you began exploring new practices.

No matter what your choices are, try to commit to spending time every day doing something that gets you just a little quieter and allows you to luxuriate in the truth of who you actually are.

We are so busy and task-oriented, distractions pull at us from every direction. But if you've been drawn to this book, take it as a sign that your inner-self wants your focused attention. Your inner-self wants to spend quality time with you.

You may explore the exercises and meditations in order, you may flip to a section that seems to point to your immediate needs, or you can randomly select an exercise each day. If you want to get the most out of your exploration, it's a good idea to set your alarm 10 to 20 minutes earlier than usual and reserve that time to be with yourself each morning. When you wake, you get to decide how to spend that time. Some days you will sing or massage your feet. Other days may be for focused breathing or yoga, meditation, quiet contemplation or a nature walk. Whatever calls you each day, allow self-care to become a habit—one you don't want to skip. No matter how busy or stressed you are, you probably make time every morning to brush your teeth. What if you made it a habit to give yourself the gift of presence?

When you begin these practices it is normal to have some agitation or feel a little anxious or overwhelmed. If you haven't had much experience listening to your inner self, it may have a lot to say at first. The experience may seem anything but quiet, still or spacious, but stick with it. As you allow these parts of you to have their say, they will settle down. You will begin to feel freer and happier than you can imagine. Just give it time and diligence. I wish you many blessings on your journey. The time spent benefiting from your kind presence is so worth it.

When this book was first a spark in my mind, my main purpose was to create an easy "user manual" for exploring feelings. There are so many great resources and techniques representing various realms of thought, and I began to notice that I was giving my clients this technique or that one, and I often thought it would be useful to put these techniques on paper so they'd be easy to share.

I have been a collector and a seeker throughout my adult life, and I've had exposure to many different schools of thought. Though yoga and science have been my primary avenues of exploration, I have found that many modalities and philosophies have unique methods of exploring the inner world, and each offers valuable ideas and techniques for the journey.

My intention is to provide an explanation of why learning to be with your feelings is a useful skill and how to achieve it. Additionally, I will discuss how the nervous system works, and how our emotions can fall out of sync with reality. I have gathered practical and straightforward techniques so you can discover what's best for you. These techniques can be used with or without the background information, but I recommend using the information as a guide, at least initially, as you become more attuned to your feelings and your body.

Everything I offer in this book is safe and gentle, though it can sometimes lead you into frightening or unfamiliar territory. If you start to feel any overwhelm, or if your emotions feel too big to look at safely by yourself, or if you find yourself stuck in a pattern that you can't seem to move through alone, I suggest having a good counselor to help you navigate those places. And if you feel as though you're at a plateau, want a boost in your process or are having a hard time going deeper, then getting some good somatic work, such as myofascial release, is an excellent way to help explore more deeply the held feelings in the body.

My mentor, John F. Barnes often says, "Feelings never killed anyone." That line has been a saving grace for me at times when the grief or pain was so deep that I thought my heart might actually break, or my head might actually blow up. What seemed to be true in those moments was that the resistance I had to feeling was what created the pressure. Once the resistance was surrendered, even a little bit, the energy of the emotions had a chance to express and move, freeing up energy that I had been clamping down on for most of my life. The freedom on the other side of those feelings was so massive that it was difficult to believe I had let my fear of facing myself hold me back for as long as it did. I now welcome those uncomfortable moments. Once we allow that stuck/frozen feeling to move, we feel more freedom in our bodies, more peace in our minds, and more fluidity and equanimity in our emotions.

If you tend toward repression, you can expect a temporary increase in your emotional reactions, as the feelings are just finding a way to express, but the more consistent the exploration, the less reactive you'll become. You will no longer be controlled by your emotions. Instead, your feelings will become the beautiful barometer they were designed to be.

You won't *always* know the answer or *always* follow that answer. I share this because, while I offer suggestions about getting in touch with your deeper self, there isn't a right or a wrong way. Know that you won't always hear your feelings, and when you do hear them you won't always follow them. That's totally normal, and it's totally okay. In fact, it leads you into the richness of experience, which is really what this whole journey is about. Sometimes it helps to make a bunch of mistakes and bad decisions so that you can be with some feelings you haven't felt before. These are often necessary steps to knowing how to access your inner world. But at some point in your life, you will likely decide that you want to drive the creation of your experience toward what you prefer. You will make the decision that feeling good is better than feeling bad. When you decide that, you have a wonderfully tuned instrument to help guide you toward the life that you want.

I'm here to show you that you can move forward in a positive way even if you have plenty of parts of yourself that remain scarred or unhealed. Having an awareness of those areas is very helpful. As John Barnes says, "Without awareness, there is no choice." So explore yourself, get to know who you are and admit the truth about what drives you to do what you do. Knowledge is useful, but when you become aware of your patterning, don't mistake it for who you are. Expand your definitions.

Ramana Maharshi, a respected Indian sage, posed a simple but deep question to his students. "Who am I?" If you spend even a short time contemplating this, you will clearly see that any definition you arrive at is limiting and not telling the whole story of who you are. Often we start with "I am a man/woman," or "I am (insert profession)." Expand your definition. Get bigger. As you actually allow yourself to contemplate this question, you realize that you won't find an end. Who is asking the question? Who is observing the fact that the question was asked?

Come back to remembering that you are bigger than anything you do or say. You are bigger than any ingrained pattern. You are bigger than your personality, no matter how strong it is. This bigger part of you is the part that gives you the clues and hints as to what direction feels best. You are capable of finding your way no matter how lost or messed up you deem yourself to be.

1

Getting the Brain on Board
Preparing the Mind to Listen

You Already Know

We have all experienced knowing something was "right" for us, but then second-guessing ourselves and deciding to do the opposite. We then smack our heads, and say, "I *knew* I should have done things this way."

Most of us already have a working sense of our inner compass. Some people are wide open and adept at responding to this sense. Others are barely even aware of their feelings. Most of us, no matter where we fall along the spectrum, could use some practice in heeding our inner sage's advice and acting accordingly. In fact, some finely-tuned "feelers" (myself included) often make choices that go against that inner instinct.

Learning to follow your feelings means learning to listen to what your body and your emotional heart/gut are telling you. Once you are able to recognize the cues, you can then learn to take the action that's appropriate for those cues. The concept is quite simple, but sometimes it takes a journey to get good at it.

My aim is to teach you how to access and fine tune your emotional instrument to facilitate your trust in yourself so that you can create a life that feels expansive, creative and wonderfully free.

Widening Your Channel

The yogis speak of a central energetic channel that is the path our essential energy travels through. It is the channel that connects us deeply to the earth and strongly into the heavens. They call this channel the *shushumna nadi*. For this channel to be open and clear, they speak of finding balance between the two other main channels: *pingala*, which corresponds to the right side of the body/spine, to yang or upward flowing solar energy; and the *ida*, which corresponds to the left side of the body/spine, to yin, downward flowing or lunar energy. In yoga *asana* practice, the yoga *sutras* suggest that *asana* means finding a balance between steadiness and ease, which, among other things, indicates balance between these two channels.

In scientific terms, the balance between effort and ease, the balance between upward flowing and downward flowing energies is found when there is balance between the sympathetic and parasympathetic nervous systems. (This pairing of systems, known as the autonomic nervous system will be discussed in depth later.)

Briefly, the sympathetic nervous system is appropriately activated in times of stress. This stress can be a positive and euphoric experience, such as the thrill of jumping out of an airplane or the pure ecstasy of orgasm or being fully in a moment of joy. The stress can also be driven by more negative, tragic experiences. Either way, systemically it causes your heart rate and breathing to increase, stimulates your adrenal glands to release epinephrine and norepinephrine, dilates your pupils and puts your senses and skeletal muscles on alert.

The parasympathetic system is the counter to the sympathetic system. It decreases heart rate and breath, shunts blood back to vital organs to help with digestion and reproduction, releases acetylcholine to help dissipate the excess norepinephrine and epinephrine and brings a sense of calm back to the body.

Most of us, because of our wiring and possibly our enculturation, tend to have more potent expressions of our sympathetic/stress response. The more acute the situation, the more heightened our feeling experience is. If we were accustomed to feeling our feelings without resistance, these strong surges would move quickly through our bodies. But because we tend not to give ourselves permission (or our bodies are not yet ready) to feel things like terror, anger, rage or grief fully, we hold those excess feelings in our bodies. When this happens, our systems get stuck "on" instead of having the parasympathetic response occur once the incident of trauma is over.

What we are hoping to find, just as the yogis said, is a balance between these two systems. As the intensity of experience (stress) increases, we attempt to meet that pressure with an ability to turn on the relaxation response. Practicing that balance with smaller and easier stresses can sometimes help prepare you for the big and real stresses that life can throw at you. This is how yoga and meditation practices or physical training can translate and overflow into our lives.

Have you ever noticed that most people who are regarded as heroes, saints or honored figures in history often have major obstacles or trauma in their histories?

Large stressors create a systemic overload and increased activity of the sympathetic nervous system. Sometimes this system stays on, and people get caught in a loop of trauma or PTSD, debilitating anxiety or depression that they haven't been able to overcome. The people who *are* able to navigate their way through traumas often become pretty amazing people.

One way to facilitate this kind of healing is to find a way to stimulate the parasympathetic nervous system at a level that can counter the high degree of stimulation you have endured. In yogic terms, you need to find a place of *asana*—equal parts steadiness and ease.

When these systems are balanced, the central channel is opened and widened, and our life force energy can move more swiftly and efficiently through our systems to better connect us to the cosmic force that is all around us. In short, we can feel more in yoga, or union, with all. (Some call it union with God.) Finding the balance is what seems to be the key. As most of us tend to lean more toward the sympathetic system, practices that promote ease, security and relaxation are the best medicine.

Some people prefer to stay within their comfort zone. You are fortunate if this is your default setting. Increasing "stress" through joyous, exciting or life-affirming experiences, or through athletic activities while remaining relaxed, can help such people to balance their systems and widen their channels.

As you learn to fully experience your feelings and recognize the internal signals of "too much" or "too little" in your own body, it can be quite simple to find a balance point, a place of equanimity.

The Plastic Brain

Life is suffering. This is the first noble truth of the Buddha. The longer I've been alive, the more I've come to believe there is no right or wrong way to walk on it. What there are, however, are varying degrees of ease and joy, struggle and suffering.

Some of our experiences can be traumatic enough to rock us far off center. These things are bound to happen even under the best of circumstances. We will all experience the growing pains of childhood. We will all love and lose love. We will all experience the loss of beloved people and pets. We will all experience illness. We will all feel lonely and abandoned, grief-stricken and angry and hurt at times. It's part of being human. Some of us become skilled at avoiding these feelings and even these situations by walling ourselves off, not getting too close, isolating, denying or drowning ourselves in work, addiction or enmeshing with another person. Other people allow themselves to fully feel through their entire life experience and are able to respond in appropriate, though sometimes intense, ways.

Most of us land somewhere in the middle, allowing certain feelings to surface when it seems appropriate, and suppressing them when it doesn't. Many of us lose ourselves in binge-eating or TV-watching or the internet to keep us on the surface where we don't feel too much. In fact, a case could be made that consumerism relies on us not knowing ourselves too deeply. Why would we buy the products if we recognized that we were complete without them?

We are wired to react to stimuli in a way that helps to keep us alive. The response of "fight, flight or freeze" is the biological mechanism that kicks into gear when we perceive a threat. In his book *Buddha's Brain: The Practical Neuroscience of Happiness, Love, and Wisdom* (2009, New Harbinger Publications), Rick Hanson reveals that there are more areas in the human brain focused on safety, than there are areas focused on pleasure. In nature, this serves us, as we need to avoid situations that may kill us. If we miss an opportunity for dessert or sex, we can usually find it another time, but if we don't run away from the saber-toothed tiger, we won't have another chance.

Because of our hard-wiring, our systems favor the areas of our lives that aren't going so well. In Buddhist terms, we are addicted to suffering.

At first, this knowledge can evoke a sense of doom: If this is the way it is, why bother trying to be anything other than what we are? To repeat the words of John F. Barnes, "Without awareness, there is no choice." Once we *know* that we tend to be inclined toward suffering, once we *know* that our brains default to the protective fight-or-flight mechanism when faced with danger, then we can begin to see things more clearly. After letting go of built-up habits and layers of protection accumulated throughout our lives, we can actually start to carve ourselves a new way of being. We can learn to respond. We can learn what feels good and how to redirect ourselves there.

The science world defines this ability as neuroplasticity. Essentially, with practice, we are literally able to reroute the neural pathways that carry signals to and from different parts of our brain. The yogis call the patterns that we tend toward (through learned experience or karmic mental and emotional patterns) *Samskara,* or complete action. These are the pathways that make up our conditioning. These conditioned ways of being can have positive or negative polarities. The practice of yoga is partially geared toward finding new ways of being rather than relying on our old conditioned habits. The same goes for the concept of neuroplasticity and the retraining practices associated with this type of neuroscience.

Compare your neural pathways (*samskara*) to rivers. If one of your rivers has been running its route for a long time, it's quite deep and wide. When you start to exert change upon the flow of that river, you are creating a new tributary for that water to run through. You need to dig the new river pathway deep enough to route most of the water into this new channel. What that equates to in the world of mental or emotional conditioning is practice; repeating habits until they become your default patterns. It's exciting to know that we are not doomed to perpetuate our old habits simply because they've been there for so long. Personal responsibility, however, is required for lasting change.

Given this knowledge, we are able to take back our power. The direction of our lives is placed back in our own hands. In every moment we are given stimuli, and in every moment we can choose how to perceive and respond to them. Sometimes our reptilian brain will leap into action setting off the fight-or-flight response, a more subconscious reaction that, in the moment, is out of our conscious control. When that cycle is stimulated, we have another opportunity to make a choice. We can either allow it to carry us into our full pattern of unconscious behavior, or we can slow down and bring ourselves back into the present where we can feel into the sensations and emotions that are occurring.

If the signal is too strong for us to interfere with the pattern, we can wait for the fight-or-flight moment to pass. Once the threat is gone, we can then use that information to create a more useful response.

There is no right or wrong. There is only easier or harder. Harder usually feels like a gripping or avoidance, the brain going in circles, the body in distress. Easier tends to feel more open, richer, more alive. Sometimes, feelings that are open will lead you to intense places. If it feels more alive, it tends to point us toward the path of least resistance.

Feelings Are Your Navigation System

Our feelings (or vibrations, if you prefer) provide a miraculous navigation system that is readily available to us. *All* of our feelings are indicator lights on a dashboard, even (maybe especially) the ones that we deem as unfavorable. When we are tuned up, all these indicator lights are functioning properly, and we can address whatever issues they are illuminating. For example, if we feel anger in response to a situation, we are given a signal that somewhere in that interaction we are not honoring our own need for a boundary. Once we speak up and set the limit, the anger dissipates. If we feel joy, we get a different kind of signal, and we can respond by following that joy and riding the wave that will lead us to more happiness.

For the majority of us, this dashboard has been neglected and repressed by conditioning, rules of conduct, shame, trauma and many other factors. Due to this neglect, it is constantly malfunctioning. When we repress or shun our feelings, these repressed messages build up, creating a pressure cooker of unaddressed issues.

When the anger light comes on, it comes on so strong that we can't even think before reacting. This can cause the anger to express as a dramatic reaction, an explosion directed at the person or thing that flipped the switch.

And when the joy light comes on, we are often too busy waiting for the next malfunctioning "warning" light to allow ourselves the pleasure.

This expectancy of negativity can cause us to cling to whatever turned on the joy light, leading to attachment and possibly addiction. It can also cause us to skip the joy entirely while looking for the next threat.

This journey into your feelings will help teach you to recognize what is healthy and functioning in your indicator system, and what may be overstimulated or malfunctioning. When you notice a potentially faulty indicator, I will offer suggestions and techniques that will guide you into your subconscious feeling patterns so you can meet those parts of yourself and create a more accurate mechanism.

Once your inner guidance system is tuned up and you become more astute at recognizing and understanding when and how it malfunctions, you can begin to trust your feelings. They are the most valuable tools you have to navigate your life path. Your emotional landscape is a finely tuned instrument that is designed to guide you toward things you prefer and away from things you dislike. It truly is that simple. Our logic, conditioning and belief systems can supply us with all the reasons our feelings are not to be trusted or followed. Our alarm systems can get activated by these beliefs and thoughts, and override our instinctual knowing of what is best for us. This conditioning can be very persuasive.

Finding Your Way Back to Love

There is a place inside of every being that is still and peaceful. It is a place of love. When we are centered in that place, we are completely content. All distractions of the mind and emotions are peripheral and we are non-reactive to their forces. This is the state of being that spiritual seekers try to attain through practice. It's the end game.

Most of us get glimpses of this state of being, usually during a meditation, or gazing at the stars or a sunset, sometimes in the arms of our lover or in connecting with our child, or during a peak performance of an activity that we love, when we are really in the flow. Those moments remind us that being carefree and full of love is possible. This is the place that feeling our feelings helps lead us to.

When the clear and placid lake of our being is filled with silt and the wind kicks up mud and tosses waves across the surface, or an eddy forms, creating chaos, you lose sight of that clarity and calm. Unfelt emotions and the mental chatter that fuels them are constantly tugging on your being, asking to be acknowledged. Even when you are unaware of these emotions, they are inside, waiting for the next opportunity to come to the surface and be experienced.

When you undertake a meditative or introspective practice, it is natural to start to see these parts of yourself more clearly. Often the initial stages of quieting the outward distractions of our lives and the constant rambling of our minds create discomfort. You may start to feel more anxious, angrier or sadder for a little while. These emotions have always been inside of you, but distractions have kept you from noticing them. You are beginning to dredge the lake and unearth some parts of yourself that subconsciously affect every interaction you have in your life. It takes a great amount of will and bravery to withstand seeing and feeling yourself. But if you wish to have more peace, more calm, more love in your experience, these moments of conscious discomfort are well worth the payoff. Each time you feel, you are allowing that subconscious emotion to lose some of its charge and power. Feeling your emotions helps bring them back to their natural place of equanimity—they become information gatherers rather than alarm systems. You can begin to trust that when you feel anger, your system is simply asking you to set a boundary. You can believe the sadness that you feel and know that it's simply asking you to change something in your life. The fear no longer holds you hostage. It's actually there to tell you to be cautious. Unfelt emotions produce faulty signals and create the drama of life that pulls you away from the centered self that you really are.

Emotions are not to be vilified. They are the basis of our instinct, the part of us that holds wisdom in how to navigate in the world. And when you feel fully the more difficult emotions, you also gain access to the wonderful feelings of love and joy and excitement. Emotions help us become bigger.

What's the Reward?

When we act upon the guidance of our feelings, we seem to flow more easily through the stream of life. We have more energy, our experiences are enhanced, we are more available to meet and help others. We are happier.

As I learn to point myself toward the feelings I prefer, I notice that opportunities open up and things I had dreamed about or wished for begin to appear.

The more you shift your feelings into positive ones the more often you vibrate at a frequency that feels good and, consequently, the more often you see that positivity reflected back. New doorways and opportunities might arise, smoother relationships surface, you may suddenly find "your people" in social and work environments. Your whole life opens up and flows with greater ease. The more you relax and follow those positive feelings, the more the world seems to respond in kind. Less resistance feels better. Most of us yearn to feel more at peace and more alive. The easier the flow of life, the more energy is freed up for creativity and expression. Creating and sharing our gifts is gratifying. And as you continue to do what feels enlivening, even more of what you prefer comes into your life, creating an avalanche of positive results.

Maintaining the flow of positive feelings and circumstances takes practice and commitment. You can expect to be pulled back into difficult experiences, either by unexpressed subconscious feelings/beliefs or by self-sabotage. But when you follow your inner cues, life flows and expands and you *will* feel more alive and joyful.

Because I have fallen many times, I have learned what helps me brush myself off and realign with the feelings I wish to have more of.

When you lose alignment with the joyful and positive it can feel like you are being drawn deeply into yourself, almost against your will, to experience feelings you'd rather not. This magnetic pull, however, often indicates that it *is* appropriate to look at, feel, experience and accept the emotion that's been hidden but is now seeking your attention. Emotions often don't surface until there is enough safety to do so. These moments that can feel like failure or backward motion are actually a sign that you're heading in the right direction. When strong feelings emerge unprovoked by circumstance, or if circumstance arises that reveals a buried part of yourself, try to see this as a precious offering. It may not feel like a gift at the time, but when your heart breaks and rage boils inside, or if you feel terror that was suppressed for years, this is really the path to freedom.

If you are well versed in the practice of feeling, you know that the pull of these emotions is felt physically, similar to what you feel when you are drawn to a person or a thing, but a little tighter than that. It's actually more like the pull of addiction, which is a powerful experience. Because you are simply experiencing it and not attaching action or thought to it, the power the feeling has over you dissipates. Any addict can tell you that when you feel the pull but don't act on it, it loses its charge. Buddhist meditation practices suggest becoming an objective witness to whatever you notice in your experience, to see these upsets as clouds floating by in a clear blue sky.

I'm not convinced that being human means that our experiences are supposed to be consistently positive and joyful. Part of us enjoys the ride when life gets challenging. There does come a point, though, when it feels better to have more joy, equanimity and peace. We can increasingly align with those feelings, even in the face of adversity. One of my favorite teachers, Ravi Ravindra, defines the spiritual path as an act of "moving from reaction to response." This happens when we are more centered. As we become more intimately aware of our feelings, the strength of their maladaptive pull begins to dissipate, and we get better at learning what peace, love and joy feel like. We are consequently better able to access these positive emotions when it's time to respond. If we pay attention to *all* of our feelings, we can begin to master how they express. If we suppress and stuff them, they will continue to have mastery over us, and show up in ways we don't want them to: passive-aggressive behavior, overblown emotional outbursts, or sometimes an internal simmering that leads to disease.

Once we have spent time diving into the rich and dynamic array of human emotion, and we have plenty of practice fully participating in it, feeling into the depths of those realms and tasting all those flavors, we can then choose our preferences and create a life that feels good to us.

Learning to Follow Your Feelings

When you have spent some time tuning up your emotional body, the steps to following your feelings are:

1. Sensing the feeling/vibration

2. Trusting what you feel

3. Taking action to follow what you feel

We are going to start with some basic practices to help you learn to feel and sense what your body is telling you, both physically and emotionally. Thoughts, distractions, beliefs and other things usually override the subtle cues that our bodies constantly give us. We aren't typically trained or conditioned to pay much attention to these cues. In fact, we're often taught to ignore them.

Some of us have a better connection to that part of ourselves, but most of us need some practice. My teacher, Erich Schiffman, suggests that we "practice where it's easy." In this case, the yoga mat or lying in a quiet room is a good place to acclimate to being with your feelings. The better you get when it's easy, the more readily you can take those skills into real-life experiences.

Once you get good at feeling and fine-tuning your nervous system so that the messages are clear and accurate, you then need to trust those messages. Most of us have not listened to the subtle cues our body gives us for a long time. Building trust in yourself is key.

While the trust begins to build, the final stage is to take the leap and bring your knowing into action in the world. It takes courage to try out new skills and to trust yourself enough to make changes. But in the end, you will find it's worth it.

Stress Lives in the Body

Everyone holds stress and emotional tension inside their body. When you are going through a major life stress such as acute grief, you can easily feel the ache and tightness all over. The fascial and nervous systems literally try to hold you together. Stress can present as neck and shoulder tension, hip and back pain or stomach tightness and digestive issues. Emotional stress can show up in a number of ways, build up over time and, sometimes seemingly, come out of nowhere.

Listening to what your body is telling you about what it wants and needs, and then honoring those needs, are key ways to move the stressful energy through so it doesn't get stuck. This usually comes in the form of resting/sleeping, meditating, or getting quiet enough to feel.

Another approach to tending to the body is to move it. If you're really depleted and tired, that movement may just be some gentle yoga or stretching movements. If you're anxious, a more vigorous workout that gets your heart pumping and blood flowing is probably in order. If you're stuck in a more long-term depression, exercise and movement are one of the best things you can do for yourself. Sometimes motivating to move the body takes a great deal of effort, but it's almost always worth it. And if you're not sure if your body is telling you to rest because it needs rest, or if it's telling you to rest because it's resisting feeling, just start with a little bit of gentle movement and see where it goes.

If you start exercising more vigorously and you just can't shake the fatigue, slow down or stop. Go stretch and meditate instead. The authority always goes to your body so when it talks to you, try to listen.

Exercise has been used to promote good brain health for decades. Physical changes to the brain occur from movement, and getting our blood pumping increases blood flow to the brain. Exercise releases neurochemicals that help neurons to survive and grow. It assists in metabolizing the food that nourishes the brain. Evidence also suggests that exercise plays a role in the formation of white matter, which allows parts of the brain to communicate with each other.

From a mental health standpoint, exercise releases endorphins or "feel good" hormones, so it facilitates a sense of calm and well-being. Dopamine, norepinephrine, and serotonin are increased, helping us improve focus. Physical movement releases tension in the body, which in turn decreases stress levels.

When you exercise in a mindful way, you reap even better results. Physical exercise brings you consciously into your body. As you get better at feeling what is happening in your body while it's moving, your ability to tune into what your body is telling you improves, and your mind gets practice focusing—the main suggestion of any type of meditative practice.

Yoga is a fantastic example of a physical practice that engages a focused awareness and asks us to find a place of calm and ease within an activity that might stretch our comfort zones. Any exercise will help to bring your physical body into the equation, so if you don't connect to yoga just bring mindfulness to whatever form of exercise you choose.

The Importance of Downtime

Life has become extraordinarily busy and full of distractions. We have our phones at the ready in every moment. Our families need tending to and transporting. Our work demands have increased. We schedule play dates and potlucks and family gatherings and dinners and lunches. Our days are full. When we have time to relax, we often cram it with more stimulation. We read, we watch TV and movies, we play games, or surf the internet and social media. We interrupt our conversations, meditation or exercise to answer a text message. If we're not reading and responding to email we're returning phone calls.

I am not here to preach about the evils of these activities or even place judgment on them. I absolutely love reading, watching movies, exploring the internet or a game of solitaire on my phone. It's quite relaxing if I've had a full day.

These activities, however, are *not* downtime. These are still activities that engage and stimulate the mind. True downtime is dedicated time spent relaxing and just being. If you want to learn how to have downtime, observe your cat or dog. They take naps. They sit quietly. They watch their environment and respond to it.

I don't even consider yoga or meditation true downtime, since they act as tools and techniques to help me be present in my body. While I find that I get quite a bit of information and creative inspiration during yoga and meditation, it's not the same as downtime. Sometimes people can achieve the same results through exercise or even a shower because it's as close as they can get to being quiet and listening to themselves.

True downtime is quiet time spent alone, following your own rhythm. It facilitates true relaxation and creative flow. Maybe you want to lie in bed and breathe and daydream. Maybe you'd like to take a walk and be in nature or perhaps you feel like soaking in the bath or immersing yourself in cooking a meal or petting your cat or playing with your dog. I'm referring to anything that helps you to relax into the moment without any extraneous distractions. I suggest being alone because it allows you to experience your own energy exclusively. When other people are around, it can muddle what you think and feel. How can you be sure of what you really need and want when you have everyone else's energy and opinions around all the time?

Think about the last time you spent a day completely alone doing only what you wanted to do. This is easier for some people than it is for others. Some people excel at it, but I find that most of us need practice. When you do what you want when you want, you relax. And when you relax, more of *you* comes through—more creativity, more peace, more happiness.

Nature is probably the greatest helper for us when it comes to practicing downtime. If you're lucky enough to live near a body of water, spending time near it is a great way to just be. So is watching the sun rise or set. Even spending time in your garden or with your pets is beneficial. If you live in a city, take a trip to the city park or walk around the block and enjoy the buzz of life around you. Then notice how you feel. Listen to your feelings and continue doing more of what feels good to you and less of what doesn't.

When your mind starts to spin, when your stress levels increase or you're overwhelmed and don't know what to do, try some downtime. If you're feeling dull from being on the computer all day, reset yourself. This is the easiest tool out there. Our bodies and minds *crave* these moments of stillness.

Did you know that employers are legally obligated to give us fifteen-minute breaks twice a day? Few of us ever take them! What if instead of working through those breaks by replying to email, going to social media or running an errand, you decided to *just be*? I wonder how different your day would be. What if you took your time waking up every morning, and sat with a cup of tea looking out your window at the birds instead of rushing out the door?

I know that circumstances don't always allow for these luxuries, but you always have a choice to find time for yourself. There's nothing more important in your world or your life than *you*. Practice making yourself a priority. Dare to cancel that dinner because sitting at home listening to records and dancing in your living room sounds like more fun. You don't need a good excuse to do what you want—you just think you do.

When We Can't Listen

Modern lifestyles and culture have made it exceedingly difficult to follow our instincts and body cues consistently. If you have a job or you're a parent, it's impossible to do what you feel like doing 100 percent of the time.

We have schedules and responsibilities, and sometimes those duties take a front seat to what we are feeling. We all have those mornings where every ounce of our being wants to stay in bed when the alarm clock rings or the child asks for breakfast. We have all felt a little under the weather yet dragged ourselves out of bed to do our day.

Luckily we have a pretty awesome reserve and the ability to adapt when we can't pay attention to what we know we need. New parents are the most miraculous example of resilience. When you have an infant, there's no getting out of caring for it, no matter how sick or tired you are. And somehow, despite chronic sleep deprivation and ignoring of one's own needs, you get through it. During these times the body still tries to communicate with you and with your environment. Do you wonder why a sleep-deprived mother snaps at her husband or kids? Anger is a creator of boundaries. Her inner-self knows she needs peace, quiet and sleep, even if she's unable to give it to herself.

The problem is that we can get into habits over the long term where we are *consistently* overriding our inner cues. As resilient as we are, we are simply not built to do this all the time. Eventually, we need to listen or our body's communication system. And when we don't, it will turn up the volume through illness, injury or some unpleasant way that forces us to slow down. If you're lucky, you get a virus that knocks you down for a few days. If you're not so lucky, something chronic can set in.

I am in no way implying that every major illness is a result of poor self-care. Many external factors play into illness. Long-term poor self-care, however, will most likely result in some type of expression in your body.

What can you do to be more caring toward yourself and more respectful of your body cues when circumstances aren't letting you follow your inner knowing?

One suggestion is to mindfully slow down and be gentle with yourself as you move through your day. If you're exhausted and you need to go to work, can you create the intention to slow your pace, even slightly? Can you arrange to start a little later or leave a little earlier that day, knowing you can make up the work when you're feeling stronger? If you're lucky enough to have paid personal days, would it be a good time to take one?

Parents can be really hard on themselves, thinking that they need to be present with their children constantly. But your children will get much better time with you if you get good at taking care of yourself. Can you plan a family naptime or family movie time instead of the play date you had scheduled? Can you give yourself permission to cancel the piano lesson or soccer practice, or ask another parent if your child can come over for a few hours? Can you go to a park and sit in nature while your kids run around and burn some energy?

Try to get creative with inserting just a little extra self-care into your day. Maybe the day ends with a bath, or you schedule a massage. I often tell my clients that it's okay to be busy and to have a lot on your plate, sometimes. But know that those are the times you need to increase your level of self-care. I usually suggest that my clients see me more often if they know they are overdoing it. They can spread their visits out and see me less often (or not at all) when they are living a more balanced lifestyle.

The main thing to remember is that sometimes it's okay to override your body cues. It's just not healthy or sustainable to do it regularly. If you are constantly fighting your needs, it's a pretty good indication that something has to change in your lifestyle. If you're working so hard that you can't afford to give yourself a day off, what can you do to improve your financial balance? If you're being superwoman and doing all the housework and child rearing while working full-time, how can you give yourself a break? If you're depressed and lethargic, can you change something externally to lift your energy a little and shake things up?

And when you are in a situation where you're simply unable to do what your inner self is asking, remember to come back to your breath and into the present moment as often as you can. The present moment has energy and life and vibrancy. And it helps you get into alignment with what's actually happening.

What Keeps You Stuck?

Once we become pretty good at understanding our feelings, the biggest barrier to utilizing them boils down to fear: fear of disappointing others, fear of not making ends meet, fear of not being loved. Sometimes we fear that things won't work out if we don't intervene, or we're afraid of making a mistake. The list goes on and on. Ask yourself what fears prevent you from doing what feels right for you.

People-Pleasing

If a friend asks you to help her with something, and this favor would leave you feeling depleted, it's very tempting to override the "ugh" you feel when she asks. We are conditioned to put our own needs on the back burner because being a "nice person" means doing things for other people even if we don't want to. This is deep conditioning. It can feel like we are selfish and unkind if we don't say yes every time someone asks for assistance.

In my experience, if I override my "no" feeling, I end up being resentful toward my friend and angry with myself for not paying attention to my needs. When you set clear boundaries, it's easier to say yes and mean it because you've become skilled at listening to the no. We inherently enjoy being of service and helping people in need. But it's important to discern when that's actually happening from when you might be people-pleasing. Are you overriding your instincts to be liked by someone, or because you've convinced yourself that's what good friends do? Are you helping out of a sense of obligation or do you genuinely want to help?

When you get better at saying yes when you *mean* yes, you start moving with the open flow of life. You have more energy inside of you, and therefore can be more present and joyful in each moment. And that's when the magic happens. When you do what is in your highest alignment, the people around you benefit from it as well. We don't know what others are here to experience. We hold zero responsibility for their responses to our choices. They are responsible for feeling their own feelings and honoring what is best for them in each moment. Trust that when you follow your highest instincts in every moment, that it's best for everyone involved.

Making Mistakes

Another fear that tends to creep in is, "What if I make a mistake?" This primary fear tends to be the drive behind perfectionists and control freaks, which is why I know it so well! In my conditioned mind, making a mistake meant being wrong. And being wrong meant that I screwed everything up for everyone and the world was going to fall apart because I didn't calculate the spin of the earth correctly. It's laughable, of course, to see it written out this way, but that's how catastrophic it can feel in those moments. Perfectionists tend to think they are responsible not only for themselves but for everyone around them. If the perfectionist makes a mistake, everyone will be adversely affected and won't love them anymore.

The fear of making mistakes can have deep roots. In my case, it's sent me spinning in indecision, sometimes for years. The mental noise that accompanies that fear can be so loud that it completely drowns out my inner guidance system. And when I'm able to get under the noise and feel the truth, my mind is so fast to jump back in with arguments against it that I can quickly forget what the truth was.

When these moments occur, I find that I just need to let the spin happen—breathe, slow myself back into the present moment and remind myself that I *do* know the answer. If clarity doesn't seem evident, I either don't have the right amount of knowledge to make a decision (maybe the answer is "not yet"), or the choices may feel relatively equal, and I just get to pick one and try it. Maybe there isn't always a right answer.

Perhaps not having strong feelings in either direction helps prove to my psyche that if I pick a path that isn't obviously correct that the world won't fall apart. And I get to see that choosing not to choose can sometimes feel more restrictive than making a forward-moving choice that is scary or unclear.

Trusting Yourself

Another common barrier to acting on the recommendation of your inner guidance system is not trusting the information you are hearing/feeling/seeing. Self-trust can be an issue for anyone, but if you have gone through trauma, and you have had to recalibrate your feeling/sensing system, it can be difficult to know the difference between real guidance and the faulty old fight-or-flight-driven messages you used to receive.

Knowing what information to trust can be tricky, and it's one of the reasons practicing feeling more subtly is helpful. One suggestion is that intuitive feelings usually seem more open, tingly, and alive. If something is based in fear, it often feels tighter or exaggerated. If it's based on compulsion, it tends to have a tight pull of desire attached to it that's noticeably different from the open draw of intuition. And when the mind gets heavily involved in justifications, explanations or arguments, and the feeling seems to be related to those thoughts, it is most likely *not* your intuition speaking.

Everyone receives information in his or her own unique way, so your experience may feel different than mine. But use those descriptions as a guidepost in your own experiences and see if it resonates. Write down some descriptions of what fear feels like to you, or what intuition feels like, or how addiction or compulsion feels.

We have not always been encouraged culturally to listen to our inner knowing. As children, we are constantly told to shut down our emotions. We are given messages like "big kids don't cry" or "don't be a baby" or "buck up" if we are sad or afraid. As for anger, forget it. That emotion is pretty much a punishable offense in most households.

Even if the feelings are positive ones, culture still implores us to "be realistic" and "not live with our head in the clouds." If we allow our emotions to take the lead from our logical mind, we are told that our choice doesn't make any sense.

It might be useful to think back to the messages in your own history that have discouraged you from trusting your emotions. Many of those messages have crept into your belief system and may now be holding you back from trusting yourself. Remember that those beliefs aren't even *yours*. Make a choice now to let go of beliefs that aren't serving you anymore.

Cultural beliefs are systemic, and they follow us through school, adulthood, relationships and the workforce. Logic is king. Science is king. It has to *make sense* to the mind for something to be validated by Western society. It's easy to see how we've been trained to rely on our minds and logic more than the inner feelings and instincts we possess. It's understandable why we've lost touch with the part of us that knows what's best for us, the part that empathizes with other beings, and the part that reveals our true inner longings.

Logic has been heavily rewarded, and though it is beautiful and useful to have developed that part of our brain, there are other parts that deserve our attention. Our gut feelings and intuition are essential components of the biggest decisions we make in life. We don't logic our way into falling in love, or which home to choose, or which cat to adopt from the shelter. When we pick a vacation destination, profession or employee, we may weigh pros and cons, but we ultimately choose the thing that *feels right*.

The road to re-establishing a trusting relationship with your inner guidance system usually begins with a risk. You need to be willing to take the risk of following your instincts and seeing what happens. The mind doesn't like the unknown. It will discourage you from stretching this new muscle into uncharted territory because it is outside of your comfort zone. Essentially, you have to leap with both feet. Do what your instincts are guiding you toward, notice what the outcome is and discover how you feel about it. You *will* feel fear as you leap, but see what comes afterward, or in addition to, the fear. Remember that you can always adjust your path based on the new sensations you have. The worst thing that can happen is that you have a chance to make another new choice.

The more often you practice leaping, the easier it gets to trust that you're going to land in just the right place. Soon, it will seem second nature to do what you *feel* is right for you.

(TECHNIQUE) Journaling our Beliefs and Feelings

What are some early messages you received, or fears that keep you from listening to your inner voice or following your inner wisdom?

What does fear feel like in your body? How about addiction or compulsion? What does knowing feel like? Write a description or draw a picture of each of these feelings.

Distinguishing Intuition From the Mind

Intuition	Mind
• Body feels open, tingly, alive and spacious	• Body feels tight, fearful • Stomach or jaw tension • Sense of vigilance
• Gentle draw or beckoning in a particular direction • Feels "shiny" or exciting (even if there's fear around it)	• Compulsion • Tight pull of desire • Anxiety about what the result might be
• Inner knowing, sometimes incongruent with logical thought	• Feeling contains justifications, explanations or arguments
• Gentle nudging or whisper, but it feels correct	• Alarms going off • Loud and fearful inner voice

2

Resetting Your Compass
Learning the Basics

If you are completely new to the idea of coming into your body and being present with your feelings, there are some basic tools that can help you build your relationship with your body and exercise the part of your brain that holds these superpowers. The following suggestions are a sort of "Feeling 101" course that offers a gentle and simple way to start the process.

Go Gently into Yourself

I have learned the way of the emotions, mind and soul through the vehicle of the body. Myofascial Release (MFR), bodywork, and yoga are the primary avenues I have taken to my inner world. One of John Barnes' primary principles in MFR is "never push, never force." As a practitioner, my skill is to engage the barrier that is restricted and to wait patiently, being fully present with awareness of what I am feeling. I wait at the edge and allow the body to invite me in and then respond to that engagement.

If I am pushing or forcing the system, my client's nervous system starts to send out its alarms and goes into protection mode. Not only am I going to lose the battle with the subconscious holding patterns, but I can also cause an adverse reaction. As long as the principles of loving presence and steady engagement at the barrier are followed, as long as I am willing to wait and let the body lead the technique, I will succeed in accessing what I want to access. I give the body permission to begin letting go.

These same principles apply when you begin engaging your feelings. Find a way to access the part of yourself that is speaking up. Give it your presence and steady awareness, but never push, never force. The parts of us that are holding these uncovered gems have been hurt in the past. They are fragile and delicate the way a small child is. Beating them into submission or pushing them to bend to your will rarely works. Usually, those techniques create more resistance and protection. If the body is assaulted, it forms more fascial barriers or scar tissue. If the emotional body and the subconscious are assaulted, their walls get thicker, too.

Focus on the Breath

It's nearly impossible to go through life without having someone at some point tell you to take a few deep breaths, or simply remind you to breathe when something stressful happens. The entire practice of yoga is built around breathing. Meditation practices almost always suggest focusing on the breath as a way to bring you into the present moment. If you're prone to anxiety, there's a good chance that doctors or therapists have suggested that you breathe from your diaphragm as a way to calm your nervous system.

There are numerous long-standing studies that link stress to many disease processes. Dr. Dean Ornish was a pioneer in cardiology for showing the undeniable link between stress and cardiac health, as well as offering a way to halt or reverse heart problems using yoga and meditation as tools for stress reduction.

Breathing happens here and now. When your awareness is on your breath, you are not engaged with thoughts and memories of the past, nor are you worried about the future. You are simply here, present in your body.

If the idea of breathing doesn't sound all that glamorous to you, perhaps looking at the original Western origins of the word "breath" will help inspire you. In Greek, "pneuma" means breath, but it also means "spirit" or "soul." In Latin, the word *spirare* means "to breathe," and is the root of our English word "spirit." These definitions, as well as the even older Eastern concepts of *prana* or *chi*, define the breath as consisting of much more than just oxygen. It means our vitality, our life force, our energy.

The English word for breath has devolved into the simple physiological process of taking in and expelling air. Think about this more open concept of breath for a moment. Without breath, we cannot live. The breath literally animates us and defines us as living beings. Even plants breathe. Trees "inhale" carbon dioxide and "exhale" the oxygen that gives us life.

When we focus on our breath, we are focusing on the force that brings life to us and that carries away what is no longer serving us. When I started to look at breath in this way, it changed my relationship to the simple cues about breathing. Instead of just giving my mind something to do (which in and of itself is a good idea), I started to connect to the actual life-giving force the breath offers. I began to realize the potency of this gift that keeps me going every moment of my life yet gets little to no attention or affection in return. This awareness has led to an immense feeling of gratitude as I pay mind to the breath.

TECHNIQUE Focus on the Breath

Sit in a comfortable but upright position, with your spine straight but your body relaxed. Take a few moments to get comfortable until you can settle into a place where you can be still. Now begin to feel the breath going in and out of your body.

Notice where you feel it. You may feel the coolness as it passes into your nostrils. You may feel your chest or your belly gently rise and fall. As you notice the natural sensation of the breath going in and out, also notice the relationship you have with it. Are you judging or assessing how you are breathing? Are you trying to change how the breath is happening? Once you pay attention to the breath, it's natural to notice that the breath does change. Observe what is naturally happening with the breath rather than trying to change it. Your breath may be deep and strong, or it may be soft and small. Whatever feels right for you in this moment is fine. When your mind begins to wander (and it will), simply and without judgment direct your focus back to the feeling of the breath. Watch it with affection and kindness. Continue to watch each breath and when your mind wanders, gently bring it back.

Counting or Naming the Breath

Continue breathing and prepare to incorporate an additional mental tether. There are two choices I will give you, and you can choose the one that seems to keep your mind most satisfied or the one that seems more appealing.

The first option is to count the length of your inhale and the length of your exhale. Simply count how many seconds make up the inhalation, and how many make up the exhalation. Notice if your mind wants to change the number or even it out, and then drop the temptation to exert any sort of dominion over the natural breath. Instead, allow your breath to stay as natural as possible. Each time your mind loses count or wanders, gently bring it back to the breath and the counting.

If you prefer, you can use the task of naming the action that the breath is taking by silently saying "in" and "out" as you breathe. Or "inhale" and "exhale." My personal favorite is "receive" and "let go." Choose simple labels for what is occurring when you breathe and allow your mind to continue to return to those words as the breath happens. Allow the breath to lead you, rather than the words directing the breath. Our minds are used to dominating our lives, and this is an opportunity to allow your biological intelligence to lead the dance while your mind follows.

TECHNIQUE   **Body Scan**

Another basic technique for practicing sensing in the body is to perform a mental body scan. Scanning is a great technique to do before bedtime as it helps to bring your awareness into your body and slow the mind. I recommend using this technique both when you're tired and trying to sleep and when you are alert and awake so you can learn to calm the mind even if sleep is not the objective.

Lie down in a comfortable position. Feel your body being pulled down into the bed or floor by gravity. Take a couple of deep breaths and sigh as you exhale, releasing any tension you might feel. Allow your breath to return to a relaxed state. Bring your awareness to your toes. Feel your toes relax. Feel your feet relax and let go of any tension. Scan up to your ankles. Feel your shins and knees soften. Relax your thighs and your hips. Relax your pelvis and buttocks. Feel how the entire lower part of your body is relaxed. Bring your awareness to your belly and your low back. Feel these areas soften. Relax your solar plexus and your ribs, your upper back and your chest. Relax your shoulders and your neck. Feel your upper arms let go as well as your elbows, forearms, wrists and hands. Relax your fingers. Feel your entire upper body soften and relax. Bring your awareness up to your neck and your throat and feel those areas soften. Let go of tension at the base of your skull, your scalp and your forehead. Relax your eyes and feel them sink toward the back of your head. Relax your jaw, cheeks and tongue. Relax your brain. Feel the heaviness of your body on the bed or floor as every part of you softens and lets go.

Gently scan the body again and see if there are areas that can release even further. Continue surrendering to the effects of total relaxation for several minutes, soaking in what it feels like to let go.

Embodiment and Grounding

Becoming centered and grounded in the body is one of the fundamental skills that we must master in order to hear our internal cues.

When the sympathetic nervous system is activated—through stress, crisis, illness, pain or trauma, or if we have a very sensitive system—the natural coping mechanism is to dissociate and energetically leave our bodies.

Those of us who were born extra-sensitive tend to have an underlying cellular belief that being on the planet is inherently unsafe, so it can be quite challenging to ground our energy fully into our bodies. This particular skill has been a lifelong learning process for me. A coach I worked with for a while once said, "You've got it all happening, and you know how to move your energy and have mastered many skills. What you need is to get in better touch with gravity." This fully resonated with me. Finding my strength in my legs, standing on my own two feet, confidently walking forward, being methodical and practical are not natural for me. I have pretty easy access to the "between realms" space. I also have great empathy skills and a developed intuition. I have a keen mind that quickly comes up with ideas and solutions. I'm good at listening to my gut. But my pelvis and legs have required reminders and attention.

It's interesting that the cellular body needs so many reminders about the benefits of staying fully embodied and grounded. Every single time I am fully present in my body, I feel better. My mind automatically slows, and I drop easily into the present moment. I guess that's why I love my work so much. When I am doing MFR or practicing yoga, I am more grounded than usual, and all of my natural skills are emphasized. The present moment in those settings happens in a realm that I'm comfortable with, and most days it's easy for me to stay fully there.

Walking through other parts of my life has required more practice and attention. Morning meditations and yoga practices are essential to the skill of grounded presence. The more you practice something, the better your brain gets at making it your default mode.

Staying grounded and embodied also requires frequent reminders throughout the day. I'm grateful that I have the ability to feel where my energy body is most of the time. I tend to be up (as I said before) and also slightly ahead of myself, especially in my head and a little too much in my heart. If you've never thought about feeling "where you are" energetically, give it a try. A good MFR therapist or energy worker can sometimes help you get used to how it feels when your energy is somewhere other than centered in your body. Once you feel it for yourself, it's a skill you can use regularly.

Present moment techniques tend to help drop me back into my legs and the back of my body. Sometimes I need to draw my attention more specifically into the back side of my head or heart, or even to the energetic space behind my body. I need to feel my feet on the earth, or my breath in my pelvic floor. If for some reason I'm really disconnected, I may need to place my hands on that part of my body, or contract the muscles of my legs to help the connection become greater to that area.

I like to do a short grounding and centering practice in the morning before I start my day of treatments. Here's a simple one that you may find useful.

(TECHNIQUE) **Grounding**

Stand firmly on the ground. Barefoot on the actual earth is best, but you can also imagine yourself barefoot on the earth if you're inside or have shoes on. Begin by noticing (or imagining) your feet contacting the earth. Become aware of the sensation on soles of your feet and feel them meld into the earth. Feel that connection draw downward as roots do, meandering deeper and deeper into the ground. Visualize the roots extending straight down, so far that they reach the center of the earth. See the center of the earth as a liquid crystal. Allow your roots to merge with it. Feel the earth crystal energy draw up through your roots and into your feet. Allow that energy to slowly come into your entire body, the way water draws up from the roots of a plant. Feel the strength and support throughout your body.

Now feel the crown of your head open and soften. Visualize a bright light, like rays of the sun, tickling the top of your head. Feel that light slowly cascading down your body, filling every cell. See the light enter your legs and extend into the feet and the earth and roots below you. Experience yourself totally grounded, supported and held. At the same time, be open, relaxed and vibrant. Breathe these feelings in. Continue to check into how your feet feel on the ground and how centered you are.

Relaxing into the Present Moment

One of the simpler ways to become centered is to notice what is occurring in the present moment. The mind likes to take us ahead to worrying or planning for something in the future, or it can lead us back to an event that happened in the past and create emotional states based on those memories. Even if the event happened only minutes ago, we need to assess whether it is actually the experience we are having *right now*. This technique can help you find the present moment and help you re-establish a center, despite the circumstances of your life.

Whatever you are feeling, whatever vibration you are in, be aware of it and deepen your breath. You may notice judgments or thoughts coming up about the state you are in, or what you are observing. Let those thoughts and judgments just float by, as you continue to breathe. When you breathe, you are bringing yourself into the present moment. You don't breathe in the future or in the past, but only in the now. The present moment is the only place that actually exists, and therefore it is the place you want to be when noticing your feelings.

As you breathe, pay attention to your body. If you are feeling spacious and open, joyful and calm, continue to ride that feeling and relax into it more and more.

If the feeling is a little tense or restrained, or even if it's unpleasant, be there with it. And feel yourself soften and relax a little more regardless of what you are experiencing.

Relaxing is the key to feeling how you would rather feel. The tension that you feel and the judgments and beliefs that relate to your feelings create much more suffering than the feelings do. When you relax, you are able to let the energy that makes up your emotions move and flow and express. Tension and judgment clamp down and cause suffering.

Being willing to feel what is actually happening can be challenging and it can sometimes seem like work. It requires bravery and resolve to face yourself. It can feel quite uncomfortable to be in your own skin if there are a lot of feelings you have pushed down or forgotten about.

Ultimately, the joke is on us. We have a tendency to think that by trying harder or doing more that we can achieve what we desire. Sometimes, and in certain ways, this is true. But when it comes to experiencing our true nature, our soul being, who we really are, the quickest and most direct way is simply to relax, soften and let go.

As my teacher Erich Schiffman says, "When you relax, you let go of tension. When you let go of tension, you feel relief. Relief feels good." That "feeling good" is open and spacious, and is closer to who we truly are.

Letting go isn't always as easy as it might seem. I want you to think about how you feel if someone is pressuring you to do something, or is angry that you aren't doing it right, or wishes you were different than how you actually are. Those judgments and assessments tend to create more tension and cause you to grip tighter. It's not in our nature to relax or let go under such circumstances.

Only when we feel seen, accepted, loved and valued can we start to relax. Our emotions seem to respond in the same way. With pressure or judgment, a mini-war ensues. When you push to get rid of the feelings, or judge them or have an agenda (as subtle as is it may be), the feeling will put its battle armor on, and you will experience frustration at being unable to relax or soften into it.

So start by breathing, and simply coming into the present moment. Then begin feeling, seeing, accepting and loving whatever arises in your current experience. Gently ask yourself, exactly as you are, to relax a little bit more. Notice the effects of relaxation and ride the wave of that sensation. Then relax and soften even more. Ride that wave. Continue with this cycle of relaxing and feeling the effects for several minutes.

Any time you feel drawn away or pulled into thoughts, simply reconnect with your breath and bring yourself back to the noticing and relaxing process. It is common as you do this practice to see your feelings shift and change. New ones may also pop in for you to acknowledge. Have fun observing the different ways you can respond to these changes.

TECHNIQUE **Tuning into Uncomfortable Physical Sensations (Sensing)** * 🎧

Sit or lie in a comfortable position and begin to deepen your breath. Feel your mind and your energy settle into your body, like stirred up silt settling back on the bottom of a lake. Take several slow breaths, continuing to settle and quiet your mind.

As your mind and energy settle, see if there's an area of your body that is immediately noticeable. Maybe it feels tight, or a little achy or painful. Maybe there's a different sensation that is drawing you into that area. Perhaps an image of a part of your body pops spontaneously into your mind. If something is noticeable, bring your attention fully to that area. If nothing is immediately obvious, start scanning your body with your awareness and search for anything that feels tight, painful or tense. There may be several places, so just pick one that seems like a good place to start.

Once you have chosen a spot to place your awareness, try to imagine your breath entering it. Keep the breath in its own comfortable rhythm. There's no need to deepen it unless that feels right to you. With each gentle inhale, flood the area with awareness and kindness. With each exhale, assist that spot in letting go a little bit. Stay with the area using your breath for several minutes.

Notice if judgments come up or you start to make assessments about the area. Notice if you have emotions attached to that spot. Perhaps it's frustration or sadness. Allow those thoughts and feelings to have their place, letting your breath extend its kindness to them as well. Then in the next breath, bring the focus gently and lovingly back to the area of sensation, flooding it again with each inhale and feeling it let go and relax with each exhale.

After you feel that area fully for a few more breaths, allow your awareness to widen to your whole self again, soaking in the vibration of relaxed stillness.

TECHNIQUE   ## Tuning into Pleasurable Sensations

The same technique can be applied to pleasurable or enjoyable sensations as well. Once you still your mind, simply scan your body for an area that feels open, relaxed, spacious, alive. You can even place your hand there to emphasize it, or you can create a comforting sensation, such as rubbing your chest or tickling your skin.

Then take your breath and use it to bring your attention fully to that area and the accompanying sensation. As your breath and attention land there, notice how the sensation may expand or relax more. Allow the feelings that accompany the pleasure to rise up in your system. Again, try not to judge or assess what you are experiencing. Try not to cling to the sensation, but rather just let it be, let it change and send a feeling of gratitude and kindness to the area.

Using the Body as a Sensing Tool

Sometimes the easiest way to bring awareness to an area is through touch. Bodywork practitioners know this. If you want to learn how to breathe into your belly, it helps to feel your belly with your hands as you breathe. If you want to feel your hamstrings, stretching them will give you a significant amount of information. Many of us aren't even aware that we have tight or sore spots until we physically explore, either by touch or through stretching and moving.

When it comes to ball and stretching techniques, there are many wonderful resources with great ideas about where to place balls or foam rollers to access an area of the body. The range of modalities spans the spectrum from yoga all the way to diagrams of stretches on the equipment at the gym. There are videos, books, wonderful teachers, and classes. I suggest you explore any or all of these options. I will provide several of my favorite resources in the references section.

What I'm going to offer here is a meditative technique to help guide you into your tight areas using ball placement or stretches that work best for you.

For the purpose of providing an example, let's pretend you have tightness in your psoas/belly area, since this is an area where most of us have some holding patterns. Remember: These techniques can be used for any tight or restricted area and may not be in the straight plane of motion. You may need to explore within the stretch to find the best spot. The tool I suggest is a soft, inflatable four-inch myofascial ball. Harder balls are not suggested for use in the belly area, though some people prefer them in more solid areas, such as the gluteal muscles.

(TECHNIQUE) ## Using a Ball * 🎧

Lie down on the floor and place a soft, inflatable ball under your tummy where you feel tight, hard or tender. It could also be an area that feels empty and numb. For the psoas, place the ball halfway between your hipbone and belly button.

Once you locate a spot to focus on, allow your body to melt over the ball. Focus your breath and your awareness into this area. As you breathe, notice the tension level in your face and jaw. If it is easy to relax these areas, it's a pretty good indication that you can hang out here for an extended time. If you are unable to relax your face and jaw easily, this is a signal that pressing into the spot may be too intense to start with, so adjust the ball into a place that feels a little more comfortable.

Once you've settled into a spot, begin breathing gently into the restricted area, as though your inhale is washing over it like a gentle wave on a shore. As you exhale, feel the area soften and relax a little more. Become curious about what you see and feel there. Thoughts, judgments, assessments or emotions will likely come up. Allow them to be there, and feel how the accepting awareness of the breath helps enable them to move through your system. Notice the part of you that wants to run away from the sensation. Allow that part to be there as well. Be kind to all these parts of your psyche, knowing that they have had a place in your life and have served a purpose until now. You'll often feel sensations in other parts of your body, too. This is completely normal, as the fascial system is a continuous full-body system that connects everything to everything else. Continue breathing into whatever sensation arises, welcoming it all as you feel your whole body relax and soften more and more.

Lie on the ball for at least five minutes, maybe longer. If you've never used this technique before, five minutes is a good place to start. It's helpful to set a timer, so that you can fully absorb into the technique, rather than being distracted by time. If you're listening to the guided audio technique, the music will continue for a full five minutes to give you a complete experience.

(TECHNIQUE) Stretching * 🎧

With a prolonged myofascial stretch, we are not looking for an end range maximal stretch. In my experience, stretching immediately to your limit will cause you to brush past many places where you might hold tension. I am a fairly flexible yogini, and it's been very easy for me to mindlessly transition to the end range of a pose and then come back to my awareness once I'm in the pose. So I urge you to play with this technique within any of your stretches or yoga poses, even if you aren't holding them for as long as this particular method is going to offer.

In this example, instead of using a ball to access the psoas, we are going to apply a gentle stretch to it instead. My favorite way to access this muscle is to lie on my back with a yoga block under the upper part of my sacrum (tailbone), either on the lowest or medium setting of the block. Best bet is to start lower, and if you don't feel any stretch, you can raise it up a notch. If you don't have a yoga block, a large pillow can work. Once the block is placed, bring one knee to your chest and gently hold it in front or from behind with your hands. If the block suddenly feels too low, go ahead and move it up a bit. This bent leg is used to help anchor the low back into a relatively flat position instead of an arch, so you may need to squeeze it toward your chest a little more than you think.

Once you are set, slowly walk the other leg forward. As your leg straightens out, you will feel the sensation of a stretch in the front of that extended hip and thigh. As you breathe into it, bring your awareness there. Find a stretch that just starts to elicit a mild sensation. Then allow your leg to roll in and out ever so slightly until you find a line of stretch that feels like it needs some attention. Use the wave of your breath to bring in awareness with the inhale, and relaxation with the exhale. Remember to check in with your face, eyes and jaw for tension, as this area tends to tighten up when the belly is open and vulnerable. Use this as your indication to either ease up on the stretch or soften more deeply into it. Continue breathing and gently opening the area layer by layer into the front of the hip and thigh, finding increasing ease and relaxation through your entire body. It may feel good to reach the arm on the side of the stretch overhead, or you may feel like telescoping the leg out, as if someone is gently pulling on it. Wherever you explore, find a space to be still and really feel that area gently open and soften. Continue the stretch for three to five minutes, and then repeat on the other side.

* Meditations marked with 🎧 will be available to download and listen to at LisaWestWellness.com/book-audio.

3

Navigating Intense Feelings
The Challenging Parts of Yourself

When we undertake a project that teaches us to focus inward and feel more subtly, we are bound to experience more intense feelings, such as sadness, anger or fear. When a small child is trying to get your attention and she isn't being heard, she might get louder and possibly resort to doing things that would be considered naughty. She may yell or throw a tantrum. Our emotions operate in a similar manner. When we fail to feel and express our feelings, they become bottled up and shoved away while we try to forget about them and focus on something else. When these feelings have been ignored for a while, they tend to behave badly, often at moments that are not congruous with the situation in front of us. We snap at our loved ones or become fearful over small things. We get in the habit of worrying, or we become melancholy.

These more intense or negative feelings will invariably start to come to the surface, usually more easily than some of the positive ones. This section will give you tools to use when you are faced with some of these feelings. Tuning the instrument of your body's wisdom requires willingness to feel *everything* that's been stuffed inside. It requires an enormous amount of energy and a lot of physical tension to hold these emotions in. The key to navigating more intense feelings is to allow them to be experienced without letting the story about them take you for a ride. Buddhist mindfulness meditations speak of letting the thoughts pass by like clouds in the sky; we notice them, but don't grab onto them. Our thoughts and stories cannot control our lives without our attention. If we can become skilled at simply feeling the sensations of fear, anger or sadness in our bodies, while simultaneously letting go of the reasons behind them, powerful and rapid changes can occur.

Owning Your Feelings

One crucial step in traveling into your interior world is to acknowledge that your feelings are *yours*. This may sound simplistic, but it isn't always the easiest thing to do.

When someone cuts you off in traffic and you get angry or feel trapped, it's easy to project those feelings onto the driver who caused the emotions to surface.

If you're having an argument with your spouse because something he/she did or said upset you, it is easy to blame him/her for causing the pain, hurt, frustration or anger. Arguments often happen because we jump into the "you did this to me" mode in our minds.

We have become really good at justifying all the reasons we are victims of our environment. When we evaluate the situation that just happened, we can say, "A led to B and that is why I feel angry right now." But most of the time, our emotions are expressed more intensely than is warranted for the situation at hand. The level of anger you feel because the kitchen is a mess when you wake up in the morning is likely beyond the kitchen being a mess. It even surpasses a story you could add on like, "He has no consideration for me because he left the kitchen a mess and expects me to clean it up." This anger is triggered because it's compounded by the unexpressed anger from every single time you haven't felt respected or visible. At that moment of awareness you have a choice: own your anger or hold onto the story that because he doesn't do the dishes, he doesn't respect you. When you review the scenario objectively, it becomes clear how easy it is to muddy the waters and give small incidents so much power over your inner life.

There are, of course, times in your life when you are actually victimized and the feelings you have are warranted. Your anger, fear and grief are legitimate and should be honored. But even in those situations, it's important to remember that what you've endured isn't the totality of who you are. In order to reclaim your power, it's necessary to let go of the feeling of victimization and decide to step into a broader definition of yourself.

What if you decided to own your feelings? What if you were able to step out of the feeling of helplessness and simply notice that you feel anger, sadness or fear? Many times just having this awareness gives the feeling a pressure release valve. Sometimes, in larger build-ups of emotion, other interventions are necessary to help that emotion move through. But holding steadfast to the idea that what *you feel* exists solely because of someone else causes it to get stuck and build up even more. Sometimes we yell and scream and blame, and it can feel like a temporary release, but often it causes more damage, increases the anger and becomes a destructive cycle.

It can be difficult to take a breath and own your feelings in the moment they start to surge. You may fall into patterns of blame (a role brought on by fear) and you may need to "play out" the emotions sometimes. It's nearly impossible to stop the train when it's already heading down a hill. But if you take some time to reflect on the truth of the situation that's causing your anger (rather than stewing in self-righteousness), you can often begin to see the facts, motivation and trigger more clearly.

I have played out all of the roles many, many times. Most of us have at some time or another. But after we have become experts at self-righteousness, being the victim, bully or whatever part our inner child wants to act out, we eventually see that staying in those modes doesn't reward us. The "he always" and "she never" scenarios start to have holes in them.

There is no shame or guilt in playing these roles. If we didn't, we wouldn't be able to see the parts of ourselves that are crying out for acknowledgment and love. The trick is to witness what is unfolding rather than to identify with the part you just played. Become curious about why your inner child might be acting out so that your inner adult can provide the comfort she needs.

These dramatic moments help us see where we need to process our feelings, and they help us see what tendencies we have, and what feelings might need more attention than others. These moments teach us that the fine-tuned navigation system of our inner knowing might be skewed a little too much toward anger or hurt or sadness or fear. This doesn't mean that we shouldn't trust those feelings when they arise, but it does give us some insight into moments when we're unsure about taking action on those feelings. Waiting until you are calm and centered before responding is usually the right choice.

If you tend toward fear, for example, doing something that is out of your comfort zone will probably trigger a higher level of fear and caution than is warranted. If you know this is a pattern for you, then this knowledge can help you act in spite of that fear.

If you tend toward anger, you may lash out at your wife for forgetting to tell you about dinner plans with friends, and regard it as a personal assault. But if you *know* that you tend toward anger, you have the choice to own your feelings, give your wife the benefit of the doubt and have a lovely time rather than seething with resentment and having a tense evening.

Owning your feelings is simple, but it isn't easy. It requires the willingness to admit that you don't know everything, and that the filter through which you see the world might not be as clear as you thought it was. Ownership requires a level of humility that can make us feel vulnerable. It causes us to actually see that we are in control of our own experience in the world. In every moment, you have a choice to feel hurt and sad and to express those feelings, and then allow yourself to feel peace and joy. Taking responsibility for your emotions is one of the most empowering things you can do in your life.

If you have emotional trauma in your body (you do), then expect emotions to sometimes cloud your judgment. Know that working through them, using techniques offered here, receiving bodywork or somatic therapy, or spending time contemplating and *feeling* will lessen the charge of those emotions and bring you to a balance point where emotions become the navigation tools they were originally designed to be.

This chapter will be subdivided to take a deeper look at some of the more challenging emotions we experience. Though all the techniques in this book assist in quieting your mind and bringing you into a sense of calm and peace, there are certain techniques that work especially well in dealing with specific emotions. These subdivisions allow you to access these ideas easily, based on what you might be working with at any given moment.

Sadness and Grief

Sadness, like any other emotion, can come in a broad spectrum of intensities. It can range from mild disappointment or nostalgia all the way to consuming grief or depression. As with fear, this is an easy emotion for me to summon. As a sensitive person, I tend to feel deeply. And I have seen the power of allowing myself to go deep into the abyss of sadness and let the tears come.

Sadness feels heavy. It feels like a vortex of magnetic energy that draws you down and in. It's a softer and less dynamic emotion than fear or anger, and it's more vulnerable, which perhaps is why women are given more leeway to express it.

Culturally, sadness has been seen as weak and childish. ("Big kids don't cry" or "You're crying like a baby.") People are uncomfortable with sadness and don't know how to react to it. When was the last time you let yourself cry in public? My guess is if you allow sadness to move through you, it's done privately.

We are living in a country that has an ever-increasing rate of antidepressant use. In a 2011 CDC report, one in ten Americans were using antidepressants, and more recent studies have seen those numbers rise. Sadness is rampant and often stuffed inside us since childhood. Crying is our very first expression. We do it at birth. It was an outlet for all of our emotions. I think crying is still one of the most valuable tools for letting emotions flow.

Sadness and grief are paths that fear, anger, guilt and shame can take to get closer to your heart and the truth of who you are. Allowing yourself to feel the tenderness and vulnerability within you, to feel the heartbreak of the people you've loved and lost, the letting go of parts of yourself, the admission of loneliness and separation, the death of ideas about who and what you are and who you wanted to be, to feel the longing for dreams unrealized ... these are doorways into open-heartedness.

Grief, in my opinion, is one of the most powerful experiences of being human. Every time I've felt and processed grief, when I go into the depths of the physical experience and allow myself to sob and reach for my breath, and to feel the actual physical feeling of my heart cracking, I am admitting deep in my body and soul that I love something very much. Grief literally breaks your heart. It creates a crack in some of the solidity around your essential nature, and connects you more deeply with yourself and with others.

Grief teaches compassion. It nods in recognition of how interconnected we are. We are given opportunities throughout our lives to have many of these big, intense experiences of sadness. And if you notice in your own life, you will see that when grief takes hold of you, it magnetically grabs onto the residue of other past grief experiences that you haven't fully experienced and accepted.

Be grateful for grief, for without the big and powerful experiences of sadness to help us feel more deeply into our hearts, we just keep accumulating milder forms of sadness, which are harder to dive into and can sometimes build into melancholy or depression.

When the doorway into sadness is opened, it can pull you into that dense and inward place pretty significantly. Because the human body is a keen instrument of communication, when you feel sadness, it is useful to be quiet and more nurturing and kind to yourself. It's a period of "life review" and contemplation, something that modern life does not allow much time or space to do.

⬭TECHNIQUE⬭ From Grief to Relief

Sit or lie in a comfortable position. When I am really sad, I like to curl up in a fetal position. Try this if it resonates or brings you comfort. Start to breathe and feel into the place in your body where you notice the pull of sadness. Compassionately and lovingly embrace that part of yourself. Let that part know that it's okay to be sad. Give yourself permission to feel sorry for yourself. You have been hurt, and it's good to feel sad about what you've been through.

Feel what your body wants to do to express this sadness. It may want to move around, it may want to cry. It may want to wail and scream. Or it may just be a quiet, energetic feeling of slowly pulling in or opening up. Whatever you feel is correct.

Continue to notice the sensations in your body. Feel how expressions of sadness lend themselves to feelings of relief. Feel into the relief when it comes. Allow yourself to ride the wave of expansion that occurs when the expression moves through.

(TECHNIQUE) ## Shaking * 𝕆

The shaking technique can be used for any emotion, and actually helps move energy in general throughout your body. I'm placing this technique under the sadness category because sadness feels so heavy and can keep your system feeling dull and lifeless. It's especially useful if you are melancholy or depressed.

Shaking your body is one of the best ways to quickly bring more life force into your system. I suggest finding a song that you love with a good beat to play during this exercise.

Stand up and allow yourself to begin bouncing up and down gently and loosely. Allow yourself to get as floppy and sloppy as you can. Feel the looseness and vibration radiate throughout your body.

Now let your arms and maybe your legs get into it. Allow your body to shake out and move. Let the movements get bigger and more exaggerated. Let your lips make horse sounds and feel your jaw and face jiggle. Exaggerate the shaking motion throughout your body and let any sounds come out that want to come out. Shake your spine more and feel yourself getting more and more liquid. Spend a good two or three minutes shaking your whole body. If you're using music, it will provide good timing for this activity.

When you finish shaking, STOP all at once. Stand still and feel your entire body. Feel your heart. Feel around your body. Breathe, and bask in this feeling. Stay in the wave of the feeling you've created inside. Let the energy move throughout you.

Sometimes I follow this technique with a scream from my belly as loud as I can. Try this if it feels right. Then again, stand in stillness and feel the energy move through you after the scream.

It is not uncommon to find tense or tight or sore spots in your body that you hadn't noticed before the process. These are simply areas that would like more of your attention. Perhaps stretching or movement of these areas is called for, or at least time to be present with that part of yourself.

Getting Stuck in Sadness

I'm certain we've all had times when we were aware that we spent more time inside the vortex of sadness than is useful. Anyone with depression absolutely knows that feeling, and those with a low-level melancholy also know how it feels to be stuck.

Sometimes there is an actual chemical change happening in your body that is causing this prolonged state. A prime example is the hormonal changes that happen in puberty and menopause, or after a pregnancy. The chemicals in your entire system are altered. Pervasive thoughts and loops in the mind can also keep you in the sadness (or any of the more challenging emotional vibrations) longer than is useful.

It's counterproductive to think you need to be any other way than how you are, so accepting that you're stuck and acknowledging that it's okay to be stuck is a good place to start with yourself. Taking steps to resolve the issues that might be keeping you stuck then becomes a little easier.

If there's a chemical reason, it may help to address it with your doctor or naturopath or acupuncturist. Seeing an MFR therapist or bodyworker who addresses somatic and emotional issues might help you get under the feelings. A good talk therapist may also be helpful.

Don't bypass the sadness—get into it. It may linger, so be patient and tender with it. And when it moves through you, feel the open-heartedness inside and the aliveness around your chest. Feel how on the other side of the heaviness and muck is expansion, brightness and life. Bask in the vibration in your body after you cry and wail and feel. The moments of openness that occur after you allow yourself to feel deep sadness are key to getting through it.

Remember, we have biological tendencies that bias toward stasis. Sometimes sadness can keep you safe in your cocoon longer than you need to be there. So practice leaning into the feeling of openness that occurs right after you allow the emotion to move through you. Perhaps journal about *that* feeling—how it feels, looks, tastes. What inspirations are being sparked by this more open feeling? Ride the wave of feeling *good*. Practice it as much as you can. Feel the relief of letting that sadness out. Be curious and see if this practice can help you feel a little less stuck. Another useful technique for getting unstuck is "Broaden your Perspective," found in the section dealing with anger.

Navigating Through Fear

Fear is one of the most primal instincts we have. Healthy fear is what keeps us a foot back from the edge of a cliff while we're hiking. It tells us to back away from a rattlesnake. It's what's kept our species alive. When anxiety (at worst) or worry (at best) starts to creep in, thoughts fire and swirl and all the alarm systems go off in our bodies. Adrenaline is released, giving us extra energy to either run or fight. Blood diverts from the belly and pelvis to the muscles and limbs. The heart beats faster and breath quickens. Vision and other senses are heightened and we become more keenly aware of our surroundings. We are ready to face the threat.

Unlike the heaviness of sadness, the energy of fear feels more superficial, almost as if it sits above or around your body, like the hairs on your skin are alert and awake. My fear energy expresses fully in my shoulders, neck and head. My body is tense, and I lose my awareness of the ground beneath me or any feeling of solidity. I lose the connection with my belly, and my breathing seems to get hijacked into a shallow tight place.

Fear is a tricky thing. When you are functioning within a well-modulated system, fear gives you the instinctual signal that something isn't right. Something is posing a threat to your survival or your well-being and homeostasis. Fear reminds us that we need to pay attention and ask the question, "Am I okay?"

I have this imagined experience of walking through the world with an integrated, appropriate, and healthy level of fear. I see myself hearing and trusting that warning signal, and acting appropriately to address whatever is not in proper alignment. Then I continue in life feeling secure and relaxed, open and present. I know in my gut that this is how we are built. When you watch a small child or a pet that has had a secure beginning in life and is naturally laid back, this is how they respond to the world. The threat is gone, there's a short "shake it off" recovery time, then they fully re-enter the world, open and peaceful.

This has not been my experience. Fear continues to be the feeling inside that I have the hardest time trusting, because it arises frequently. My alarm system fires at a low level much of the time, so there's a constant need to return to my breath and remind my bigger, "knowing" self that it's on the right track, and that I am safe and free from the threat my body thinks is out there.

And when a real threat looms (having to move, start a new job, have a difficult conversation), my alarms start ringing at a higher volume than is appropriate and my mind gets to work trying to solve the problem. This seems like such a service, (thank you mind!) but when the mind is fueled by fear, thoughts circle and internal arguments ensue. The mind transforms from placid lake (which is ideal) to murky, stormy sea. In short, our beautiful tool that helps us solve problems and take appropriate actions turns chaotic.

When you become more practiced at learning to breathe and settle down your system in the face of negative thinking and fear, you learn to pre-empt a whole body reaction or panic attack.

When you take steps to form a relationship with your fear, and you see how it presents itself internally, you will begin to notice exactly how your fear is expressed. As I mentioned before, fear triggers a systemic biological response in the body that causes you to fight back, run away or freeze. In nature and during true threats, each of these mechanisms serves a very crucial function. Though these processes are automatic, we can insert our consciousness into the process and learn a new way to be with fear. Healthy fear is something we need to trust and follow, because our gut knows when something isn't quite right. This type of fear carries a quality of inner wisdom. It is felt more in the gut than in the mind.

When you become afraid, what is your most common pattern of expression? Looking at how you deal with conflict in relationships usually offers a strong clue. Do you tend to start yelling? Do you walk away and close the door? Do you freeze up and become unable to talk? We all do all of these at some point, but notice what your main fear response is.

I tend to freeze. When I sense a threat, I get quiet and ultra-alert. My rational mind goes blank and all I can focus on is the constant assessing of all of the information around me, waiting to see if it's safe for me to make a move again. This is almost always my first unconscious strategy. If I freeze and the threat leaves, then I can usually stay with my fearful feeling and process it appropriately.

If freezing doesn't work, and the threat escalates, my next phase is to run away by either walking/stomping off or closing/slamming the door. If this isn't an option, the fight response kicks in—yelling and screaming, defending and blaming. Once the fight response kicks in, my feelings usually shift to anger, which has a lot more power and energy behind it. Even when I progress to running away, anger starts to seep into the equation and I get a chance to feel it once behind closed doors.

I know other people who immediately move to the "action" part of fear. They engage. I actually envy these people because they have a quick outlet to dissipate the adrenaline in their bodies. When you watch a cat posture and hiss and engage its threat, you see how the built-in process is supposed to work. The cat has its conflict, shakes it off, stays puffed-up for a little bit, and then regulates its system and returns to its baseline. Most of the time, we don't allow ourselves the full expression and dissipation of these emotions, so our systems often stay in a mild agitated state rather than fully down-regulating to a place of calm and peace.

This becomes more complicated when your fear response differs from someone you are close to. If you tend to freeze or retreat, but your parent, child, sibling or partner tends to fight, processing that fear energy in the moment becomes quite challenging for all concerned. When this happens, it takes discipline and practice to accept personal responsibility for your biology, and to honor the other person's process.

Perhaps you recognize these tendencies in yourself or in a loved one. (It's much easier to see patterns in others.) I'm the one that people perceive as giving them the silent treatment, as I am utterly unable to engage when I am in purely fearful reaction mode. ("I'm frozen. Leave me alone to process this.") And when my boundaries are violated, then anger, the boundary-setter, moves in to help create the space I need to be with my feelings.

I am continuously navigating my relationship with fear, so even as I share my knowledge about feelings and listening, discerning and following what feels correct, I am extremely humbled by my continual learning of this process. As we dive into what fear is, where it comes from and how to process exaggerated fear, we are able to hear the healthy information the fear is offering. I can only share what I have learned and continue to learn about my own experience with this emotion.

Fear versus Excitement

We are wired to perceive any change as a potential threat, so fear will come up in our bodies even when the change is positive. When I feel this type of fear, a certain level of excitement or anticipation about the event usually accompanies it. Those feelings are closely connected to the actual sensation, which is why people feel a thrill at amusement parks and horror films. This fear feels subtly different from the warning signal type of fear, and it takes a little practice to sense the difference. There is a part of you that knows what you are changing is good for you, even though your mind can make a compelling argument about all the reasons the change may be disastrous. The pivotal moments in people's lives tend to involve risk and moving outside of comfort zones. Practice feeling that fear/excitement connection and notice how it is different from the warning fear that keeps you from harm. When you experience the purity of the vibration of fear in your body, you will notice that it is a similar vibration to that of excitement. Fear is like excitement but without the breath and positive anticipation, so it constricts your system. Because these emotions are similar to each other, because they are two sides of the same coin, we can use that to our advantage to help flip our perspective.

Fear and excitement are a reaction to change. Mild excitement or fear can happen with things like trying a new food or going to a new place. More extreme feelings tend to occur with bigger events like bungee jumping or moving to a new city. We usually have both feelings present when reacting to change. The next time you feel fear coming up around a situation in your life, see if you can start to let the grip and tension relax a little and ask yourself, "How is this situation increasing the excitement in my life?" Start to look into the adventure and the thrill of a new experience.

Sometimes changes are thrown at us—our house is foreclosed or we need surgery or a family member is dying. Life presents us with changes that feel anything but exciting. These times call us to experience a whole gamut of feelings that aren't necessarily welcome. But occasionally hope arises; you have graceful moments when you know that whatever is happening is bringing you into a new realm of experience, and you realize that you will get to the other side of it.

Challenging experiences remind us of our resiliency, and show us our strength and adaptability. They push us to our edges and stretch us further than we ever knew we could be stretched. We learn that we can survive, and sometimes we learn that we can thrive and find grace, even under enormous stress. Through challenging experiences, we get to see how awesome we are.

When Fear Cries Wolf

When you begin observing your fears you will likely see that many of the messages are habitual thought patterns rather than actual in-the-moment threats. Because the mind is so actively engaged in the fear cycle (after all, fear only happens in the future, not in the present moment), it can be helpful to give the mind a little soothing balm before moving your awareness into the body. One suggestion is to ask yourself what the worst-case scenario would be. When you watch the tailspin in your mind (which usually ends with "and then everyone dies") it can help to lighten your mood a little and laugh at the creative places the mind can go. Perhaps the answer ends up being something more rational and you realize that everyone dying is unlikely to happen. Be proud of your creative and active mind, and allow yourself to relax a little bit with this game.

Once the mind is soothed, you can start to process the fear. I notice that some mornings I wake up in a small buzz of low-level fear or tension, so I use one of these techniques to allow that subtle anxious energy to relax and unravel.

(TECHNIQUE) Feeling into Your Tension Level

The following is a technique that I have adapted based on my studies of meditation with Erich Schiffman. His shared awareness about meditation suggests that the only thing you must actually do in order to feel the connection to your inner self is to relax the tension in your body and pay attention to the results of relaxing. This technique can be used at any time no matter what emotion you are addressing, but because the feeling of fear is one of increased tension, it's a great emotional state to practice this on.

Sit or lie in a comfortable position. Begin to slow your breath and connect your breath with your body. You may feel the expansion and contraction of the lungs. You may feel the air in your nostrils. As you breathe, notice areas in your body where you are holding tension. With each inhale, fill the tension with kind awareness. With each exhale, feel the tension soften and let go a little bit. Notice the gripping on the surface of your body and skin. Feel the tension around your body. Use the same breath awareness in the areas around your body. As you feel the areas that are holding tight, start to let go and feel the relief. Ride the wave of that release and notice how it feels spacious and good. Continue to breathe. Continue the cycle of noticing tension, relaxing it a bit and feeling relief.

From a vibrational and neurological rewiring standpoint, the feeling of relief and open, spacious joy is key. Linger in that sensation for as long as it lasts, and notice that you can summon that feeling through the simple act of relaxing tension.

(TECHNIQUE) Letting Gravity Win

Fear is an ungrounded experience. Our energy goes up into our heads, out in front of our body in a state of vigilance and protection. This technique will help you settle and reconnect your life force to the center, lower and back side of the body. As the energy settles into these places, you will feel your sympathetic system let go and tension levels reduce.

Sit or lie in a comfortable position. It may help to place a heavy blanket over you. You can assist this process by using the weight of your hands on your body. Imagination works, too, but physical sensation is particularly useful. Become aware of your breath and feel yourself slow down into the present moment. Gently place your hands on top of your head (if sitting) or over your forehead and eyes (if lying). Soften your hands and connect gently with your head. Feel the soft weight of your hands assist as your eyes, face and brain slowly settle into the pull of gravity. Soften and breathe as your head continues to get heavier.

Slide your hands to your shoulders (if sitting) or chest and diaphragm (if lying down). Allow your hands to soften and relax. Feel the gentle weight of your hands as they touch your body. As you connect with your body, feel gravity start to gently draw you closer to the earth. Feel your internal organs drop deeper into your body, letting go of tension. Let yourself get heavier and heavier.

Finally, slide your hands onto your belly, hips or thighs. Soften your hands and connect lovingly with your lower body. Breathe into this area and allow the weight of your hands to assist in getting heavy and settling in to the earth. Feel the organs of your belly and pelvis sink back and down. Allow the pull of gravity to extend into your legs. Feel your bones get heavy. Breathe.

(TECHNIQUE) **Present-Moment Joy**

One of the quickest and easiest ways to shift out of fear and calm your system is to bring yourself into a joyous present-moment activity. (When you get really savvy, you can just summon the feeling of present-moment joy.)

Feeling the breath in your body is a good way to assure you are present in the moment, so this will remain the suggestion for slowing yourself down and coming into the now.

Find an activity or a place that you know brings you peace, calm and joy. Some suggestions are petting an animal friend, sitting or walking in nature, listening to music, or simply looking around at the natural world all around you. (Even in cities, you can find trees, plants, birds, etc.)

Decide to take a few minutes (or longer if you have the time) to engage in your favorite present-moment activity. Connect with your breath and allow your senses to be receptive. Quietly look around. Feel the air on your skin, the fur of your pet, or the grass or sand under your feet. Soften your ears and notice the sounds around you. Really feel your senses becoming more alive and alert.

Allow yourself to feel the relaxed joy of being present right now in an environment that brings you peace and happiness. Let the feeling of that relaxed joy fill your cells with every breath. Allow the tension in your body to relax and soften so even more of the moment can seep in. Give yourself permission to feel good *right now*. Luxuriate in this moment for as long as you can. Let the feeling linger and ride the wave.

Insecurity

Thinking you are not good enough can sabotage your life in constant, small ways. Insecurity can set in, no matter how much I have to offer, how many people love me and what I do, or how many of my clients notice improvement. Sometimes insecurity is situational, like those moments when you teach your teachers (or in my case treat people who I consider gifted geniuses at what they do). Other times, it just comes as a moment of doubt, seemingly out of the blue.

If insecurity strikes while I'm working (because my work involves being pretty much in my connected "feeling" side of my brain, and because I have enough evidence at this point to know that I'm good at what I do), I am simply reminded how the mind can hold onto false beliefs and that insecurity just wants my attention, again. These are moments where it's fairly easy for me to practice what I preach, and watch the thought and the connected body sensations just float through without attaching to them.

A more difficult scenario involves being in a social setting where I am out of my comfort zone. I can be talkative and open and have easy conversations with many different types of people one-on-one, but I find being in groups more challenging. When I am in a social setting and insecurity shows up, I have a tendency to hide the fullness of who I am. A part of me doesn't believe what I'm saying is worth being heard. That part wonders if what I'm saying is stupid or is concerned that it might reveal information that will cause the group to exclude me, or that I might upset someone. If I'm not vigilant, those old, faulty beliefs can sabotage the expression of who I am.

The Value of Insecurity

As social beings we rely on each other to survive and thrive in the world. We want to contribute and feel valuable. Remember that biologically we are built to desire stasis. When we are stretching our boundaries a little, our biology has all sorts of ways to communicate discomfort, and warning signals will be sent out if something isn't within the margins of our comfort zone. The voice of insecurity is a presentation of the fear of rejection, which to a social being can feel like a threat to survival. This burst of fear may, in certain cases, be valid. You may be feeling insecure about sharing something personal with someone who isn't a safe person to do this with, for example. Insecurity is the social presentation of the same biological warning that you would get while assessing whether you can jump across the stones in a river. It's the doubt and the pause that helps you make sure that you have the ability to proceed without hurting yourself. But often, when that spark of social fear is lit, it gets turned inward. The mind takes the warning and starts spinning an old tale that reinforces feelings of unworthiness. Most of the time, insecurity is simply not useful.

We are bombarded with the "I'm not good enough" message in Western society. Advertising is absolutely based on this message. "If you buy our product, you can be whole, more beautiful, more manly, stronger, healthier, happier. You can be *better*." Society stays functional based on this message. People stay in low-paying jobs that they hate because they don't think they are capable of doing something else or worthy of being paid more. Unfortunately, we have linked our survival to commerce, so the survival instinct will often win out over the knowledge that we deserve more in life. Many of us have looked at the stones across the river, and have determined that they are just too slippery to navigate safely. The information we are getting that leads us to this prognosis might be correct. But it also might not be. Be willing to explore how much your self-esteem, self-worth and capability are involved in your assessment.

Letting Go of Faulty Beliefs

Because the physical and emotional responses to insecurity and low self-worth are created by our inner dialogue and old belief patterns (such as guilt and shame), it may be useful to question them. They don't always offer concrete, valid information about our environment.

As you start exploring your own inner world of feelings and sensations, notice if any of these messages are attached to "I'm not good enough." If those words create a recognizable sensation inside of you, it's likely that part of you is holding onto a belief that isn't yours, and simply isn't true.

If self-esteem or confidence is an issue for you, I suggest writing down some of the old beliefs you may still hold around not being good enough. Think of any phrases you were told (or told yourself) as a child that might still be in your psyche. Once you bring the light of awareness to those beliefs, see how those beliefs make you feel inside, then next to each of those faulty beliefs create one that feels better—write a new story and start exploring. Affirmations are a nice thing to use, but if you really want to carve out a new way of thinking and being, add in the sensation and feeling you get when you say or think the new words. "I am a wonderful mother. The love I have for my children is more than enough to raise them well." What does that feel like? You can try, "The work I do is valuable and helps make other people's lives better." Breathe in the feeling of value, joy and confidence. Notice the expansion that comes from seeing yourself in a new light. Get good at feeling that way. It may be more difficult to connect to those positive sensations at first, or it may even feel like you're lying to yourself. But keep practicing, and over time you will see that those feelings get easier to access and you will start to feel and see the truth.

TECHNIQUE Journaling Suggestion

Draw a vertical line down the center of a piece of paper. Ask yourself, "What are some of the faulty belief patterns that are holding me back or keeping me small?" Write these down in the left column. Then, in the right column, create a positive affirmation or replacement belief for each of them. Embrace the feeling of each new belief and breathe into the associated feelings for a full one to two minutes to help create new patterns.

Anger: The Great Boundary Setter

Most of us have an unhealthy or not fully integrated relationship with anger. Depending on your upbringing, you have either learned to use it quickly and often as a response to a perceived threat, or you have learned that it can be destructive so you haven't accepted it fully into your experience.

When you begin working with the energy of anger, the power and strength behind it can feel a little scary. Anger holds a lot of life force, so it's a good idea to make friends with it.

My history with anger amounted to learning to stuff it. This seems to be the case for most people I know. When we are toddlers and playing with this emotion for the first time, we throw tantrums and say "No!" to anything we don't want to do. We stomp and hit and bite and cry and scream. Our little bodies are becoming acquainted with the power of this emotion and are learning about physical space and individual desires. We are learning for the first time to take care of our needs, but in a forceful and demanding way.

Obviously, this creates chaos for everyone around us, and it's not a pretty way to function in adult society, so most parents teach their children not to behave this way. It's maddening to be around a toddler who is flailing on the floor and carrying on because he couldn't press the elevator button.

Because toddler outbursts defy logical human interaction or civil rules, we learn pretty quickly that mom and dad do *not* like it when we express these strong feelings in such dramatic fashion. We learn that expressing anger is often met with more anger, shame, disconnection, punishment, disappointment, guilt, or any other number of emotions from the people we rely on for our sense of safety and of self.

Many of us also learn saying no doesn't do us much good either. "No" is a healthy expression of anger. It is a clear boundary. When we are two or three years of age, we sometimes set these boundaries at times that aren't appropriate for whatever is happening around us. But if our no is consistently ignored, we learn to stuff it, too.

As we grow up, it becomes apparent that when we abandon boundaries to do what makes our parents happy, we tend to get better results. In some very real ways, this prepares us for the world and how society is set up. It's extremely useful to be adaptable, learn to compromise and to have somewhat malleable boundaries. What's unfortunate, however, is that many of us end up blurring the edges of our own needs to the point that we lose sight of what we want or what healthy boundaries are.

The levels of stifling anger vary quite a bit by gender and upbringing, of course. Little boys are often given more leeway with anger. Historically, it's the only emotion that society deems acceptable for men. Anger creates strength and allows men to go to battle. Little girls are generally less encouraged to express anger or boundaries of any sort. They are labeled as "bossy" when they say what they want. And as teenagers they become "bratty" or "bitchy." These labels have negative connotations, so most girls try to avoid being labeled these things. The anger then gets stuffed every time a boundary isn't set, or our wants and needs are unexpressed and unfulfilled.

The end result is (and can we ever see it playing out in the world) a lot of people have a lot of anger that has built up over a very long time. Because it hasn't been felt, acknowledged and expressed in a healthy way, anger leaks out in outbursts or in passive-aggressive behaviors, depending on the permission you've given yourself to start communicating your dissatisfaction.

Our aim is to integrate anger into our experience and learn to use the energy to create appropriate expressions of what we want and need, what we expect, what we deserve and what we won't tolerate. We learn to use it to be energetically firm when setting boundaries.

The process of transforming excess anger starts with being willing to acknowledge that it exists and allowing yourself to feel it. Again, this is a powerful emotion, so it can sometimes seem scary or overwhelming when it starts to move through you. The expressions that come out are usually loud, physical, strong and from the gut. The energy that releases is *big*. We feel energy around us, and with a strong force like anger, it's quite apparent. When someone around you is angry, the entire environment changes, like a knife slicing through the air or a bomb exploding in the room.

I highly suggest that when you start tapping into this emotion you give yourself ample space to express. Being alone in your house in a room where you will be undisturbed is a good idea. Once you start feeling the anger come up, it's useful to work with a trained professional who specializes in somatic expression. MFR is my go-to modality, but there are many other methods that work with releasing emotions in the body as well.

The suggestion and techniques I will offer here are simply the ones that I have found to work best for me. Feeling your feelings as fully as you can, without the need for your mind to talk about "why" has been the most direct route for my own processing of emotions. It doesn't mean I don't have room for talk therapy or journaling—I do those things quite a bit. My mind loves knowing more about my experience, and those things often settle the dust enough to allow me to drop into the feeling more easily, especially when it's strong and almost overwhelming. But pure bodily expression is key to full integration.

Feeling into Anger

An ideal way to feel into any feeling is to drop immediately into it when a trigger occurs. Sometimes circumstances make this difficult. Usually, I need to take space for myself after the trigger happens.

Find space to process as soon as possible when a strong emotional reaction occurs. This space could be your room, your parked car, somewhere in nature—whatever feels safe for you.

(TECHNIQUE) ## Softening Around Anger

Sit or lie in a comfortable position. Deepen your breath with the intention of settling into your physical body. Notice how your body feels as you do this. Often I feel as though all my energy is at my upper chest and head and extends above and beyond it. I feel my jaw tense and my eyes sharply focus. I feel my chest puffed and my breath shallow. Sometimes my fists are clenched. You may experience different sensations. Take note of what you feel.

Once you notice the feeling, allow your breath to soften those rigid and tense areas. Observe what happens to the sensation when you begin to soften. Perhaps you feel the surge of aliveness that the tension is holding in. Perhaps you become aware of your belly and pelvis or you feel a sound wanting to come forth or a desire for movement in your arms or legs. Soften more. Allow that energy to move through your body. If you can, let the expression release.

Screaming into a pillow can work. Punching your bed, or allowing your body to go into a full-on tantrum may be in order. Other times, you can just feel the surge of energy moving through you. Sometimes your arms or legs might tingle. Sometimes tears will come. Sometimes the movement is subtler.

Whatever you observe, *feel it.* Then breathe and soften some more. Feel it. Allow it. Express it.

Once the intensity has moved through you, stay in the aftermath. Can you feel the warmth in your belly? Can you feel the strength? Sit in the vibration of the powerful being that you are. Continue to breathe and soften into this wonderful feeling of being alive.

Facing the Shadow

We live in a culture—both legally and religiously—that sends us the message that when you do something "wrong" you will be judged and punished in order to restore balance to what is fair and just. Most of us hold this belief pretty strongly, often without realizing it. With the advent of technology and social media, culture has become louder, and contempt and judgment are part and parcel. News headlines continue to fuel the fires of anger and self-righteousness. We are encouraged to speak out and act out in violence. (Yes, even derogatory comments in social media can be violent.) We are constantly whipped into a frenzy over our causes. No matter how morally correct they may seem, if they are based in judgment and anger, we are perpetuating an energy that does not accept our shadow parts.

Similarly, the events transpiring in the world can feel overwhelming and depressing. Rather than becoming despondent, be grateful that we can clearly see the things that aren't working. Through my own shadow work, I have come across qualities that I would rather not see or own as parts of my psyche. These previously hidden qualities can no longer be ignored. These times in history offer an amazing opportunity for us to open our eyes to what is broken and how people are hurting. How we decide to respond is the crucial action step that each of us is asked to take.

These reflections on societal issues give us opportunities to see our own shadow in the face of perceived injustice, fear and anger. We get to experience all of our deeply buried feelings and express them. We may meet these shadowed parts with resistance and reactivity. Some of us burn down buildings and march angrily in protest or throw hateful comments toward the people we view as the enemy. Some of us seethe and speak angrily to our friends about what's wrong with the world, and blame and judge harshly the actions of others. We get in touch with the self-righteous defender of our deepest fears and wounds. And we will fight tooth and nail to keep the enemy "over there" instead of seeing that the enemy actually lies within us. The pain of admitting what we wish was not true is too much for most of us to bear. Who wants to actually own their contempt and hatred? Who wants to admit that they have murderous rage or paralyzing fear silently motivating their actions? It's not easy to see our lack of trust in life or another.

We also get to dive deep into the dualism of "us and them" and "right and wrong." It's much easier to stay on the surface and see others as the problem and ourselves as the victim or savior. Our ideals and outrage create a gap between ourselves and others and, even more tragically, a chasm between the aspects of ourselves that so want to be integrated and accepted as the full expression of who we are.

All spiritual traditions speak of returning to love—some call it heaven, others call it oneness. If we truly want to return to love, if we truly seek the kingdom of heaven, we must learn to bridge the gap between our idealism and our dualism. If you find yourself playing the external blame game, work with it there. How can you find humanity in the enemy? What would activate your compassion? How can you access just a little bit of understanding about why they are the way they are, and why they do what they do? Is even a little forgiveness possible?

If you are masterful at punishing yourself and meeting your own wrongdoings with judgment and shame, how can you find compassion for yourself? Help to bridge the deep divide between what you see as right and wrong, good and bad, us and them by realizing that every single being on the planet (including yourself) has the entire spectrum of possibility within them. Until we learn to respond to each other and ourselves with love, that divide cannot be bridged.

Because the Bible largely influences the Western world, we have access to a good example of tolerance, union, compassion and forgiveness in Christ. You don't even have to believe he existed in order to gain the benefit of the stories of his life. It can be complete truth to you, or it can be mythology, but the message is the same: Love and compassion win over violence and hatred. There are no exceptions to what is forgiven and who is afforded compassion—even those who are violent and/or hateful.

Kindness During the Process

When you begin to look within and face your various shortcomings, it can be difficult to be gentle with yourself. The standards you hold to yourself might be loftier than what you expect of others. I have a tendency to judge myself quite harshly when I realize that I've been unkind, or when I feel my anger escalate to judgment, hate and contempt. This observation of negativity in myself is compounded when guilt and shame get piled on top of qualities that are really just begging for compassion.

This is where kindness and forgiveness can come into play. Learning to forgive others and myself for the things I deem wrong or not "positive" is a process I have yet to master.

The part of me that has not yet learned to accept and forgive my shortcomings and human struggles is the same part that sabotages my life. Rather than forgive myself and move on, I will subconsciously punish myself in order to feel restored. As I become aware of this tendency and see that the real redemption comes from self-acceptance and compassion, these tendencies begin to fade.

Learning Kindness and Forgiveness

Increasing your capacity for kindness and forgiveness is something that takes practice. All parts of our psyche can be made louder or quieter based on how much attention we give them. Remember, neural pathways and habits are formed through repetition and dedication. If I were to recommend just one area for focused practice, it would be in the realm of kindness and forgiveness.

These practices can target general areas or specific qualities of yourself that you judge or disapprove of. They can also be used with an external villain—someone who has wronged you or sparks feelings of anger or hatred.

When an aspect of my own psyche has been activated by someone else's "transgression" I have found great benefit in making it the focus when practicing the next technique, which expands the feeling of compassion, no matter who or what the subject is.

(TECHNIQUE) Tonglen Meditation * 🎧

I am offering a rendition of a Tibetan Buddhist meditation practice called *Tonglen*. This meditation style helps cultivate compassion and kindness toward the self and others. There are many variations on the wording of *Tonglen*, depending on where you learn it, but the essence remains: Cultivate feelings of kindness and love toward the subject of the meditation. I recently sat with a Buddhist nun who told a story about a lama from Tibet trying to teach the *Tonglen* meditation to a group on the East Coast of the U.S. Traditionally, you begin with sending the positive thoughts to yourself first, then to people you love, and finally to people you have a harder time with. The lama found that Westerners struggled to cultivate kind feelings for themselves, so he had to reverse the order and have them start with someone they loved before turning the kindness inward. Keep this in mind if you are struggling to feel kind toward yourself. You may need to start with a pet or a loved one.

Sit or lie in a comfortable position. Begin to feel your body and become aware of your breath. Now picture in your mind, either yourself (or an aspect of yourself) or another person who has created some feelings of love within you. As you hold that picture in your mind, connect more deeply to your breath. As you inhale and exhale, repeat the following words in your mind:

Inhale: "May you (I) dwell in my heart"
Exhale: "May you (I) be free from suffering"
Inhale: "May you (I) be healed"
Exhale: "May you (I) be at peace"

Repeat this mantra and feel yourself cultivating the sensation of loving kindness inside yourself. View the subject of your meditation as you would a dear friend or a sweet child, someone who could benefit from extra love. Continue repeating this mantra until a general sense of well-being and compassion wells up in your heart.

Then slightly shift the mantra to:

Inhale: "You (I) dwell in my heart"
Exhale: "You are (I am) free from suffering"
Inhale: "You are (I am) healed"
Exhale: "You are (I am) at peace"

Repeat this mantra a few more times. Feel your compassion and resonance with that vibration grow and become more solid and grounded in your energy field. Let the kindness expand outward toward all beings.

Once you finish this step, bring up an aspect of self or others that you dislike or feel some anger about. Repeat the exercise using that aspect or person as the subject of the meditation. Extend positive feelings of compassion toward them as you repeat the mantra.

When Anger Feels Overwhelming

Sometimes an emotion can be so loud and so big that it's easy to feel swallowed up by it. You can lose your sense of being bigger than the emotion, and it can be rather scary to engage with it. Because anger feels so powerful, it often overwhelms us. Other emotions like fear or sadness can also swallow us up, so the same technique offered here can be used anytime you feel like engaging the emotion is too much, or if you can't seem to see your way through it.

(TECHNIQUE)   **Broaden Your Perspective**

Sit or lie comfortably. Take a few breaths and feel into the emotion that you are experiencing. Feel the sensation in your body, see the color if there is one and notice any other input that the emotion is giving you. Imagine that you have a camera and you are zoomed all the way into the feeling, like an extreme close-up. Take a few breaths while being with the emotion in this way. Feel the sensation in your body.

Now, slowly zoom out from the inside of the emotion. Pull the view back further and further until you can see the edges of it. Pull back even more, until the emotion is a small shape on a large canvas. Notice how much of what you see is something other than this emotion. Continue to zoom out until that emotion becomes a mere speck on the broader picture, like a single drop in a vast ocean. Allow yourself to feel the distance from the emotion and breathe. Let your body feel the relief of being out of the intensity, and allow the stillness of the bigger picture remind you how big you really are, and that this emotion, no matter how compelling or loud, only occupies a very small part of the entirety of you. Breathe and rest in this feeling of relief.

Guilt and Shame

Guilt and shame are perhaps the most self-destructive feelings to carry. These are feelings that we add on and attach to actual experiences we've had.

Healthy guilt happens pretty quickly (sometimes even before the event that causes the feeling). It is an inner knowing that we acted in a way that wasn't in alignment with what is right. Our inner compass tells us when something we did doesn't feel right, and gives us information about how we might respond to a similar situation in the future. It's the nudge that leads us to apologize or move in a direction that feels more open and loving—closer to who we are. When we feel badly about something, it can be useful for a short period of time because it gives us this good information for future reference.

Shame, an even deeper and more destructive emotion is an assessment that because of how we have acted, we are not worthy of love.

We learn shame and unhealthy guilt through our upbringing and society at large. From the time we are very young, we are shown our mistakes by other people. In an effort to teach empathy and right behavior to our children, we often end up (either inadvertently or intentionally) using guilt or shame to highlight the activity that we deem unacceptable. We try to give our children a moral compass and provide them with a glimpse of what their inner voice may say whenever they make a mistake. An unfortunate side-effect can be that instead of learning empathy (I see how the other person feels and am sad that my actions made them feel bad), the child will often turn those experiences into guilt or shame (I made that person feel bad and therefore I am a bad person).

We convince ourselves that we are not worthy of love and happiness. We allow past mistakes to define us and create our future. These feelings hold us back from being our best and brightest. Instead of forgiving ourselves, as we would forgive someone who made a similar mistake, we continue to punish ourselves for something that happened in the past. We throw a net around our energy field, keeping ourselves contained in a tight little shadow of what we could be, because we feel we deserve to be small and restricted. We forget that mistakes are simply life experiences—events that teach us what feels good and what doesn't. Instead of learning from our mistakes, we use the shame as a tool for self-punishment.

Long-term guilt or shame keep you stuck in a small version of yourself, and in order to let them go, you must make changes in your belief system about yourself. Yes, you need to acknowledge and *feel* them, but these feelings move through your system much more easily once you decide that the beliefs that created them no longer serve you, and you make the decision to forgive yourself.

Guilt and shame work under the assumption that we think we know what's best for others and that our actions are the cause of others' feelings. We over-inflate our role in someone else's life, rather than step back and see a bigger picture. Maybe the apology you offered after the mistake was one that the person desperately needed to hear from someone else and didn't get. Maybe it led to a deeper healing. We simply don't know. Once we realize that we are merely having a human experience on this planet, and that we are here to learn and to grow, we start to have a broader perspective. Making mistakes is a part of this process.

Do big mistakes change you? Of course they do. Sometimes they provide the pivotal moment in your life that will completely alter its course. And sometimes we end up hurting people in unimaginable ways. But there is a difference between attempting to make amends and punishing yourself by holding tightly to guilt and shame.

Self-hatred is simply not useful. What *is* useful is to feel into guilt, shame, and self-hatred, and to see what you are holding onto underneath these belief-inflicted emotions. Usually, when you start exploring, you'll find an enormous amount of grief. It *hurts* to feel unlovable and to withhold love from yourself. It is wildly painful to keep yourself in a cage of self-inflicted darkness.

If you look at some of the more amazing bright beings you know, I'm sure you'll find that their histories have brought them through some brutal times, and that their pasts are littered with huge mistakes and possibly even regrets. But what they have decided to do, what has allowed them to shine so brightly, is to forgive themselves and allow love in.

When you withhold love from yourself, you dim your light. That doesn't just harm you; it withholds your light from everyone else. It hampers the necessary full expression of your being. The world is screaming out for more love, more kindness and more forgiveness. If you're unable to learn to forgive and love yourself, how will humanity be able to?

This is not intended to pile more guilt and shame on you for having these feelings, but rather to point out that there's a bigger picture at play. Our myopic view can sometimes keep us stuck in our own dramatic life to the point of forgetting that, in the larger scheme of things, we need to learn how to love more. We need to practice forgiveness and grace and kindness. These are the qualities that help our light shine more brightly. Guilt and shame do the opposite. No one treats us as badly as we can treat ourselves. Start being kind to *yourself.* Make the choice right now to forgive yourself for things from the past. Make the choice to remember that you are a beautiful and loving person, and you are worthy of feeling this way. Let love in.

(TECHNIQUE) ## Let Go and Forgive

Sit or lie in a comfortable position. Begin to deepen your breath and bring your awareness into your body. Allow yourself to relax and let go of tension with each breath.

In your mind's eye, bring up an image or a memory of something for which you have felt guilt or shame. Notice where in your body you are holding this pain. The memory will often cause something to tighten and pull inward. It may feel like a giant thumb pressing into your energy field. Notice what it feels like and be present with that discomfort. Breathe.

Ask yourself if all of the beliefs around this feeling are completely true. See if that inquiry can create a little bit of doubt around the conviction you have had about yourself and this situation. See if you can loosen the grip of your mind.

As you allow more space into the experience, try to soften even more. Feel into the relaxed softening. Other emotions may come up, or they may not. Allow yourself to be present with whatever arises.

Now ask yourself, "Am I willing to forgive myself for what happened?" Sit with this question and the feelings in your body as you ask. Visualize yourself loosening the grip around the situation and slowly feel yourself soften and open. Tell yourself, "I let go of this. I forgive myself. I no longer need to carry this around."

As this energy releases, feel the light and space that can come into your field. Allow it to fill up every cell. Continue to get softer and softer, and allow yourself to feel more space, more light, more love. Stay in this energy for several minutes.

I recommend repeating this technique often. When you notice that the guilt, shame and self-hatred are lessening or not there at all, and as you get better at feeling the expansiveness of love and forgiveness, these are good indications that you have worked through those particular beliefs and your body now knows your self-worth.

4

Nurture the Nervous System
Learning to Relax

Most of us have layers of exaggerated emotions that cloud our judgment, making it difficult to trust what we are feeling. Many of us hold some degree of trauma in our bodies. Sometimes the trauma has a physical origin such as a past accident or injury, and sometimes the trauma is more emotional. Even if we can't pinpoint a major life event that may have caused trauma, many of us have a hyper-vigilant nervous system, and we hold a layer of anxiety or fear around living. Learning how to soothe and calm the nervous system is crucial. A heightened system will create false alarms and warn of threats that aren't actually dangerous. The fight-or-flight response paralyzes us, keeping us from moving forward and living to our full potential. As you let go of the excess tension that you carry around, it becomes easier to understand the truth of what your feelings are trying to tell you, and easier to trust and follow through on the messages you receive.

In order to recalibrate your miraculous inner guidance system to a baseline that you can trust and follow, you must first tend to your autonomic nervous system. Finding a way to self-regulate is the primary action necessary in order to get your feeling sense tapped back into your deeper wisdom. In layman's terms, you must learn to relax!

There are many scenarios that can bring your system out of balance, and over-stimulate your fight-or-flight mechanism. Pain, illness, trauma, threat, stress and an overactive mind can all kick your survival mechanism into gear and dominate your decision-making.

Some of us have had this system in overdrive for so long that it has become stuck in "on" mode and has manifested in ways like panic, anxiety, depression or rage. Many of us are in a low-grade alert mode much of the time. Think about how you feel after you watch the news, for example. "Fear this. Be angry about this. Be sad about this." Your survival system is reminded that threats may exist, and responds by kicking on. Even if it is only a slight increase, it can affect your ability to maintain the levels of peace and calm you deserve.

We all have times where we could use a tune-up to our inner navigating system and we could all benefit from spending more time in our parasympathetic (relaxed) state. When we are relaxed, we are in the present moment. We seek out happiness and pleasure. We are able to make good decisions based on good internal information. When we are relaxed, we feel more loving. We have room for compassion and kindness and tend to expect the best out of people. We can bond with others and with our environment. Relaxation is our natural state, where we can feel our connectedness with everything else and remember the truth of who we are.

Working with the Physical Body

Because your body houses your stress, a critical part of your recovery and integration process involves connecting with the body and moving it. Any sort of physical exercise is useful, but yoga synchronizes the mind, breath and body. The breath occurs here and now, and it helps to tether the mind to the place where your body resides: the present moment.

If yoga isn't for you, paying attention to your breath or the physical sensations you experience as you use your body can transform any exercise into a more mindful practice. For example, if you like to swim, you could count the strokes between your breaths. You could feel your arms pulling through. You could feel the kick through your legs or feel your heart beating as your blood pumps. If you're a runner, feel your feet as they hit the ground, or your breath quicken as you exert more. Feel your shoulders and arms relax as they swing through.

(TECHNIQUE) Physical Technique: Half-Sun Salutation

If you haven't done a mindful physical practice like yoga before, this is a simple way to start bringing focus and feeling into your body as you move. Moving mindfully through a half-sun salutation (a hatha yoga staple) is something most people can do without much difficulty, as long as you don't have back issues that keep you from bending forward. I will lead you through a quarter-salutation first, and then move to a half-salutation. If the half-salutation feels hard on your body, stick with doing a few more quarter-salutations. Tethering the breath and the mind to even simple movements creates huge benefits.

Stand in a comfortable but upright posture. Feet can be together or slightly apart if you need more balance. Have your arms resting at your sides. Take a few breaths. Inhale as you bring your arms up above your head. Exhale, and bring your hands down, palms together at your chest, then sweep them down to your sides. Inhale, reach the arms up. Exhale, bring palms together at your chest. Repeat a couple more times, feeling your arms expand and reach on the inhale, and your body settle back in on the exhale.

Next, let's move into a half-salutation:

1. Inhale, arms up

2. Exhale and swan dive forward, allowing your knees to bend, reaching toward the ground

3. Inhale, slide your hands up onto your shins and flatten your back, looking forward

4. Exhale, fold forward letting your head drop

5. Inhale, bend your knees slightly and use your legs to help bring you all the way up to standing, reach up above your head

6. Exhale, hands together in front of the chest

7. Repeat this sequence once more, feeling your body expand and reach more with each inhale, and relax and settle with each exhale

Stand again, arms at your sides and simply notice how your body and essence feel after moving in a mindful way.

The Nervous System Explained

The nervous system is complex, but can be defined in simple terms as the brain and nerves, or expanded to include the neuromyofascial structures at a cellular level that make up our entire being. I will give a brief overview of some of the main areas of the body that cause us to react to stress and trauma. Trauma can be held anywhere throughout our fascial system, but the limbic system, autonomic nervous system (ANS) and enteric nervous system (ENS) are the players that we know the most about when it comes to regulating the fight-or-flight and relaxation responses.

The Limbic System

The limbic system refers to the part of your brain that lies in the midline around the hypothalamus, and is involved with emotion and memory and with keeping balance.

This is the area of the brain that is responsible for instinctual emotional responses such as fear, pleasure and anger, and the area that controls primal impulses including hunger, sex, dominance and caring for our young. It also houses long-term memory and the olfactory (smell) system. This area is sometimes referred to as the "feeling brain," our subconscious, or what Barnes calls "Channel 3."

The limbic system helps control our visceral and autonomic nervous system responses. This is important in the context of feeling, because the messages that the nervous system and viscera (gut) give us are part of the body-speak that we are tuning into and taking cues from. If the limbic system is maladapted and causing us to bias more toward the fight, flight or freeze response, we are often getting faulty messages that aren't actually in line with what is best for us.

The function of the limbic system can be further divided into specific areas:

The **hippocampus** is primarily responsible for spatial memory, the type of memory that helps you navigate and orient a location or a maze. It also controls new learning and short-term memory, mostly concerning things that can be explained in words (explicit memory).

The **amygdala** is responsible for memory, survival-related decisions and emotional reactions. It is highly associated with stress responses, emotional learning and in mediating emotional and behavioral arousal. An event with a strong emotional response often creates a stronger memory for that event. This is an area that tends to be enlarged in people with a trauma history.

If the amygdala is stimulated, it creates behavioral reactions and can lead to rage. Though the amygdala responds to many different emotional stimuli, anxiety and fear have the strongest influence on this area.

The amygdala also impacts what is known as episodic-autobiographical memory (EAM), which is the memory of the "who, what, when, where and why" of events in one's life. It also records the emotions associated with that memory. Sometimes "episodic learning" can occur where an association with the memory creates a conclusion based on that experience. This is one way that traumatic experiences can get stored in the brain. For example, if you have a memory of being frightened from missing a step on an escalator when you were a child, you may develop a fear of escalators based on that memory. You may rationally know that escalators are safe and that the actual likelihood of being hurt by another escalator may be low, but the fear happens anyway because learning and memory are stored and activated in that part of the brain.

As a side note, there are some theories that a larger amygdala may also correlate to increased creativity. Though we can't say a large amygdala *causes* creativity, it may be useful to know there is a positive side if you happen to have experienced trauma that led to increased amygdala activity, or if you are naturally predisposed to higher reactivity.

The **hypothalamus** is the part of the brain that strongly influences sexual function, the endocrine system (hormones), and has a major role in the function of the autonomic nervous system (ANS) responses. It receives input from the hippocampus and the amygdala and sends signals out to the brainstem and spinal cord for ANS regulation. The hippocampus also controls temperature regulation, appetite and circadian (sleep) rhythms.

The limbic cortex of the brain is the **prefrontal cortex**. Once we start talking about cortexes, the brain functions are more complex. This area receives input from the amygdala and other areas of the limbic system and relates to mood, judgment and insight, as well as conditioned emotional responses. Damage to this area can affect mood and create tactless behavior. This area is strongly affected by alcohol use and also contains the cortex for smell (olfactory cortex).

The Autonomic Nervous System

The autonomic nervous system (ANS) is the system that stimulates involuntary (or automatic) reactions. This system includes the sympathetic nerve fibers (fight-or-flight) and the parasympathetic fibers (rest and digest). The ANS controls things reflexively that help keep us alive, things we couldn't possibly use our "thinking brains" to control all the time such as blood pressure, heart rate, breathing and digestion.

The signals from the organs, sensory areas and muscles and vessels of the body arrive at the medulla, pons, and hypothalamus of the brain, and signals go from these areas of the brain back down through sympathetic and parasympathetic nerves to each of those areas.

The parasympathetic nerves (PSNS) derive from cranial nerves three, seven, nine and ten. Along with some sacral nerves, they send messages to the eyes, gastrointestinal system and other organs. Some of the normal functions of the parasympathetic system are to reflexively constrict the pupils if a bright light is shined into them, to start digestion when food enters the stomach, or to tell us that we need to urinate or defecate. This area also causes the dilation of the cervix and contractions of the uterus during childbirth. We have limited ability to voluntarily control some of the parasympathetic reflexes.

The sympathetic nerves (SNS) travel down the spinal cord to cluster into ganglia in the area of the thoracic and lumbar spine, where they then travel along blood vessel pathways to different areas of the body. These sympathetic nerves then relay reflexive responses to dilate pupils, increase heart rate and blood pressure, increase respiration and constrict digestive function. Some other responses of the SNS are to dilate the blood vessels on our skin and stimulate sweat production on a hot day, and to stimulate the tone in our blood vessels to keep blood from pooling in our legs when we are standing (and cause us to faint). The sympathetic system is more automatic and we have little volitional control over it.

The adrenal medulla (in the center of the adrenal glands) also contains a bundle of sympathetic nerves. The adrenal area is what releases adrenaline (epinephrine) into the bloodstream and synthesizes norepinephrine.

Healthy Autonomic Nervous System (ANS) Regulation

When you are presented with a stressful trigger, one where you feel fear, your sympathetic nervous system gets activated. When you are faced with a threat, your body goes into fight, flight or freeze mode. Your blood shunts to the big fight-or-run muscles, goes away from your digestive and reproductive functions, and puts your system on alert. Your senses are more acute, and adrenaline is released to help give you the quick energy boost that you need to react to the situation at hand.

In a normally functioning ANS, once the threat is gone, your body shakes off the excess adrenaline and your parasympathetic system takes over. (Think of an animal that just got into a fight—it shakes to release the excess hormones and trauma). Your blood pressure lowers, heart rate decreases, blood goes back to the digestive and reproductive organs, and chemicals are released to counter the adrenaline that the SNS triggered.

Enteric Nervous System

The enteric nervous system is the part of the nervous system that resides in the lining of the gut. It is referred to as "the second brain," as it responds to most of the same stimuli that the brain does and it can operate completely independently of the higher brain. The gut lining can learn and record information just like the other brain does.

The enteric nervous system, or gut-brain, is the area where the majority of brain chemicals (serotonin, dopamine, norepinephrine and neuropeptides) is manufactured and resides. There are more neurons inside the gut than anywhere else in the body other than the brain.

The brain affects what you feel in your gut, and the gut affects what you experience in your brain. The brain and enteric system are connected via the vagus nerve. This connection is what tells the gut how to respond during a fight-or-flight scenario. For many years, it was believed that the vagus nerve primarily instructed the gut what to do when the brain sent out signals. Now we are seeing that what happens in the gut (both in feelings and in microbiome health) affects what happens in the brain. In fact, 90 percent of the nerve fibers that make up the vagus nerve actually travel from the gut to the brain, not the other way around.

The gut-brain is able to operate independently from the higher brain to help with digestion. Newer theories are suggesting that this system is also primarily responsible for moods. Researchers are also finding that certain systemic disease processes correlate to serotonin levels produced in the gut. There is still much to be learned about the enteric nervous system, but it certainly seems to play a major role in feelings, fight-or-flight responses and the immune system. It would explain the wisdom that's found in "gut reactions."

The Vagus Nerve

As mentioned earlier, the vagus nerve, or cranial nerve 10, is one of the sets of cranial nerves of the PSNS, and it primarily controls regulation of the parasympathetic responses in the lungs, heart and digestive tract. The vagus nerve exits the brain from the medulla oblongata and travels down to the larynx, lungs, heart and into the organs in our gut. It is responsible for communication between the gut and the brain, and for stimulating a PSNS response. This means that when it fires, it counteracts the fight-or-flight response. The heart and breathing rates slow down, and the digestive system begins to work again. Many of us tend to live in a more stressed, sympathetic system-dominant state, so stimulating the vagus nerve becomes a key tool to relaxing. Most of the nervous system and breathing techniques directly affect the vagus nerve.

Pelvic Floor and Autonomic Nervous System (ANS)

The pelvic floor refers to a group of muscles and fascia that create a sling at the base of your pelvis that supports the internal abdominal and pelvic organs of your body. The muscles run between your sacrum and tailbone to your pubic bone and out laterally to the sitting bones. The urethra, vagina and anus all open through this sling of muscle and fascia.

The pelvic floor has a vital relationship with the ANS and if issues arise in this area, especially in cases of pain, addressing the fight-or-flight state is important. The sympathetic and parasympathetic nerves that go to the pelvic floor emanate from the lower spine and sacrum and affect the musculature of the pelvic floor as well as the muscle that contracts to assist urination.

The sympathetic innervation of the pelvic floor muscles can cause the pelvic floor to contract, even if there is no voluntary contraction of the muscles, and it is especially prone to do so because the pelvic floor supports the pelvic and abdominal organs. This interconnectivity means that stress and trauma in the body often have a direct correlation to having too much tension in the pelvic floor muscles.

The sympathetic tension phenomenon happens throughout the body, but I want to highlight the pelvic floor because it's almost always an issue with people who have chronic pain and increased sympathetic firing throughout their bodies, though it's not always painful or obvious. Because this area is often forgotten about or not discussed in the general public or even the general medical communities, I want to bring attention to the fact that this part of the body is affected by stress and trauma, even if the trauma had nothing to do with the pelvic floor.

If you have a hard time feeling grounded or centered, pelvic floor awareness and relaxation can assist in reconnecting you with your legs and the earth.

The breath is one of the best ways to reconnect with the natural state of pelvic floor tension and help decrease the sympathetic holding in that area. The natural way for the breath to move is that as you inhale, your diaphragm and your pelvic floor both drop toward your feet. As you exhale, the diaphragm and pelvic floor slightly elevate. The "tube" of your core body moves up and down with each breath, much like an automobile piston.

Many people have a faulty breathing pattern, either from increased stress and fight-or-flight or from holding the belly in or clenching the buttocks on a regular basis. Almost without exception, people with pelvic floor issues (or bladder issues) have a breathing dysfunction and clench their buttocks muscles. Another bad habit that affects the pelvic floor is sitting in a slumped position (you are on your sacrum instead of your sitting bones). Awarenesses of these alone can change people's lives and have a great impact on their healing.

If you have pain in your pelvis and hips, or problems with bladder health, it's a good idea to work with a physical therapist and a skilled MFR practitioner to help address these issues. Even if you don't have pain or bladder problems, the pelvic breathing exercise that follows, is very effective for calming your nervous system and stimulating the vagus nerve.

Pelvic Floor Awareness and Breathing

This technique is the best go-to for any level of tension or anxiety. It is the starting point for many of the other techniques, and is a great way to simplify when you just need to get back to basics. I highly recommend making pelvic floor (or low belly) breathing a staple that you bring into your daily life. At birth (barring trauma at birth), we breathe in this manner. Watch a young child or baby while they sleep. Their belly rises and falls rhythmically. Many of us get into the habit of holding our belly in. Stress, allergies, smoking and other factors can cause us to breathe into our upper chest instead of defaulting to the pelvic/belly breath when we are at rest.

⬭ TECHNIQUE ⬭ Pelvic Floor Breathing

Sit or lie down in a comfortable position. You can have knees bent or legs straight if you are lying down. If you choose to sit, make sure you are on your sitting bones and not on your sacrum. Place one hand below your belly button. Picture a balloon in the center of your pelvis. As you breathe in, feel this balloon fill up with breath and light. Feel your hand rise gently as you do. As you exhale, watch the balloon slightly decrease in size, but keep it filled with the image of light. Inhale and feel the balloon fill up three-dimensionally. See it. Exhale and feel the balloon reduce.

If you are having a hard time feeling the breath extending down to your pelvic floor and feet, you can bring your knees toward your chest, or squat to help increase the sensation in the pelvic floor.

Keep the breath calm and easy, even if the visualization shows the balloon expanding quite a bit. Continue with this visualization as you feel your whole body relax. Notice that as the balloon expands, the pelvic floor gently drops. Notice as you exhale, the pelvic floor gently rises up. If you feel areas of tension as you are breathing, inhale and see the light washing into that area like a wave, and then back out as you exhale. You may even see the light radiate out toward your hips and down your legs a bit.

If at any time as you are breathing you feel your system tense up, or you feel agitated, drop the breath technique for a bit and allow your body to recalibrate to the change of oxygen. When you are relaxed again, gently reintroduce the visualization.

Continue this breath technique for several minutes until you feel your system calm and relaxed, and you have a good connection to your pelvic floor and your breath. Feel the relaxation and overall sense of calm throughout your body.

(TECHNIQUE) **Warm Fuzzies**

This technique is a simple one and is borrowed and adapted from Rick Hanson, a psychologist and author who specializes in positive neuroplasticity. Its purpose is to allow your brain to be filled with the chemicals that create happiness and calm. You may want to set a timer to give yourself a good five to ten minutes to soak in the feeling. Our minds can grow bored when we are feeling good, so sometimes it helps to time it out.

Lie in a comfortable position, either in a fetal position or a more vulnerable position, such as lying on your back. Breathe. Now, picture a person, place or thing that you love very much. Perhaps it's a specific memory of a moment when you felt so much love. Maybe it's picturing a pet or holding a baby. Maybe it's a place that brings you calm joy. Choose something that feels very easy to love, and let go of guilt if that moment or thing isn't your spouse or child. Keep it simple and pure.

Now feel that feeling of love that you have for that moment. Let that feeling fill your whole body. Allow yourself to smile and light up. Make the picture even clearer and allow the feelings to be intense and brighter. Feel how your body relaxes in that love. Continue to breathe and enjoy this feeling.

(TECHNIQUE)　## Gratitude

When I notice the vibrations of different emotions in my body, the one that feels the closest to love is gratitude. And it's so simple because there are countless things to be grateful for, even when your whole life seems upside-down. It may be more difficult to access thoughts of things you appreciate when your mood is low, or your nervous system is on alert. But if you spend some time thinking about what is going right, you will be able to tap into the feeling of gratitude.

Sit or lie down and breathe. Land in your body and come into the present moment. Notice your surroundings through sight, hearing or touch. Your eyes can be open or closed. Think of something you are grateful for and feel into that gratitude. Let that moment of recognition of how fortunate you are become wider and allow it to open up inside you. Summon another thing you feel grateful for and let that feeling expand. Continue going down a mental list of things you appreciate, and feel the wide-open feeling that gratitude creates. Spend several minutes in this activity. The more you sit in the vibration of gratitude, the more open you feel, and the more practiced you become at feeling good.

5

Trauma

When Your System Malfunctions

We have all experienced trauma. Some people have horrific stories and have faced huge obstacles in their lives. Others have had accidents, illnesses or surgeries, and all of us have had traumatic emotional experiences that left scars.

I spent years negating traumatic experiences from my youth, because I hadn't experienced awful abuse or tragic loss as many of my peers had. I didn't think I had any right to feel as deeply as I did, and I denied what was actually occurring in my body. I didn't even realize that I had trauma until many years after I had started eating again. Somehow, even this extreme expression of trauma didn't register that something inside me was crying out to be felt and addressed.

It's interesting that when you talk to someone who has been through difficult experiences, it's common for them to brush past it and think it's normal. When I first met my partner, he reminisced about events from his childhood, thinking they were experiences that everyone had. I would listen with wide eyes and shock as he told me about experiences he thought were commonplace.

When someone has had a traumatic experience (or multiple small traumas over an extended period of time), the amygdala is overactive, and the pathways to their thinking brain are compromised. They perceive danger when there is none, and they have less ability to plan and appropriately resolve the situation that is causing their brain to overreact. It's important to realize that trauma creates a very strong neurochemical reaction that overrides the ability to rationalize your way out of it. When someone is in a trauma response, they can't think as well as they normally would. They will act irrationally because the reaction is oriented toward survival and bypasses rational thought.

Until the trauma is released from the system and new neural pathways are established, a person with trauma will default to survival mode whenever they feel threatened.

Trauma held in our bodies can cause us to get faulty signals from our emotional knowing sense. In a well-calibrated system, your gut feelings are the messengers of right and wrong in the environment and they are an accurate instrument for navigating you through life. When trauma is held in the body, and your nervous system is in hyper-alert mode, those signals are often faulty and may alert you to danger when there isn't a real threat present.

There are many techniques to help deal with trauma. Because I specialize in the body and myofascial release, I am partial to using it to help reintegrate and release trauma from the system. The techniques used in John F. Barnes' myofascial release are designed to address physical restrictions and pain held in the body. They are essential to accessing the subconscious holding patterns that the nervous system has set up as a necessary barrier to feeling the depth of the trauma you have experienced. As you become ready to thaw out and feel the emotions and sensations that you've kept buried, over time these restrictions become unnecessary.

MFR has given me a safe way to dive into the parts of me that were uncomfortable or numb. Through this path, I've been able to release layers of pain, tension, fear, grief and anger that I didn't even know were subconsciously controlling my life. As the tension dissolved, the receptive, intuitive and sensitive nature of my true self has had a chance to emerge. Instead of being gripped by the need to control my environment, I have begun to trust life.

There are also some amazing new findings happening in the science world regarding neuroplasticity and techniques that literally rewire the brain. One of the best-known studies was done by Dr. Brian Knudson at Stanford University on a group of monks. Through meditation they were able to modulate their amygdala and limbic systems, changing the actual way their brains worked. Some exciting results are happening with programs such as Eye Movement Desensitization and Reprocessing (EMDR) or Dynamic Neural Retraining System (DNRS) that are showing real changes in the way the limbic system operates. Peter Levine also has a highly successful method of working with trauma held in the body.

New scientific studies are showing the malleability of our brains. Facilitation of the formation of new pathways requires awareness of old patterns and beliefs. We need to be willing to adopt healthier habits and convictions, and be disciplined enough to regularly practice better ways of being. Trauma and memories are held in the cells of the brain and the fascial system of the body. Notice what happens physically the next time you are startled. Your entire system seizes up, creating a whole-body response. This is an example of the fascial system responding to a threat.

What happens when we have less tension in our fascial systems and practice healthier beliefs? What happens when our new patterns and ideas have as much strength and conviction behind them as our faulty beliefs did? With focus and practice, these pathways and patterns can start to change.

Chronic Pain and Illness

There are few experiences that can bring you to your knees the way chronic pain and illness do. I am extraordinarily blessed with robust health. I have had mild injuries and small pains that would be considered chronic by the pure definition, but in general, my body cooperates with me. Though I experience my body in quite a physical, sensory way, most of my challenging moments have been in the emotional realm. I may experience great intensity at times, but my physical body has, for the most part, been a strong ally for me.

Because of the nature of my work, I meet a large number of people who have been living with chronic pain or illness. To feel constantly depleted and uncomfortable and miserable is one of the most wearing things a person can go through. When I have stress in my life, these people who are heroically facing a daily physical struggle are reminders of how blessed I really am.

Many of the issues that I see in my practice are the "invisible" chronic problems. Things like neck or back pain, migraines, Lyme disease, chronic fatigue and fibromyalgia, irritable bowel syndrome, thoracic outlet syndrome, systemic arthritis, and a myriad other issues that cause people to feel sick or in pain much of the time.

People with these problems often appear to the outside world as if they are okay, which can add to the psychological stress of the people suffering. These problems are diverse in how they manifest in the body and in their causes, but they have one thing in common which is the thing that brings them to me—their chronic problems are wreaking havoc on their nervous systems. The pain creates daily micro-trauma that causes the body to either stay stuck in fight/flight/freeze mode or to be easily triggered back to it fairly regularly.

We don't know if the nervous system dysregulation was present prior to the pain/illness or if it happened as a result of it. What we do know is that it needs to be addressed in order for people to find their way back to health.

Much like emotional trauma, physical trauma (especially repeated trauma) gets stuck in the body, so even after the threat is gone, your system acts as if it's still there. For example, I've known several people who have received treatments for Lyme disease. Unless the disease was caught and treated right after the tick bite, each of them had more healing work to do and still felt sick and fatigued for quite a while after the Lyme was gone because their bodies and nervous systems held onto the trauma as an appropriate response to the threat.

People with chronic pain may present with no structural reason for the pain. The joints may no longer be pinching on the nerve; they may have had surgery that "fixed" the mechanical problem. Of course, there may be significant physical fascial restriction that is causing the continued pain, but sometimes it's simply that their body is still in alarm mode and holding on subconsciously because it feels the threat still exists.

If you have experienced a chronic illness or chronic pain, then you know the frustration of going for test after test hoping for a diagnosis to prove you're not crazy. You're *not* crazy. And depending what the issue is, you may actually be better off *without* the diagnosis, even though it gives you peace of mind. For example, once someone tells you that you have fibromyalgia, you may feel some relief at having a direction to go and knowing that there's a name for your experience. But on a less positive note, you might start to believe there isn't much hope for you because the common thought is that you can only learn to cope.

I'm going to take the risk that comes with being a dissenting voice and challenge the traditional medical model by saying that I believe healing is possible. I've seen healing happen even in the face of "doomsday" diagnoses that render little hope. I've seen people release trauma from their bodies, sometimes to dramatic effect, while they are experiencing it. As long as your body believes it's under attack, it will continue the exhausting and health-zapping fight against the threat.

If you are suffering from a chronic illness or chronic pain, don't give up. Yes, you have medical and physiological issues that need to be addressed. Yes, what you are experiencing is very real. And if you also look at and address your nervous system as if it's been through hell and back (it has), you may start finding some new pathways to health and healing.

Explore MFR and other modes of trauma work as an avenue toward a more optimal healing experience. Some diseases may not fully resolve, but the pain and suffering most certainly can change. Let yourself be at least open to the possibility that your health can improve.

Meanwhile, from an emotional perspective, honor every single feeling that comes up as you're going through the process. Let yourself feel sad, hopeless, angry and raw. Let yourself honor the fatigue and pain and give your body all the love you can muster. When you are in your darkest moments, be the one to lovingly embrace yourself and allow the emotions to express. You deserve to feel loved. You deserve to be healthy and whole. Let it flow out as fully as you possibly can. Then breathe and feel the vibration of the space you've created for yourself. Crying physiologically stimulates your vagus nerve and creates more peace and relaxation in your body. (So does laughing, so give that a try too!)

Make sure not to skip the most important part of feeling your feelings: the after-effect. Spend time basking in the relief of letting go of that extra tension. Let the feel-good chemicals surge through your system and let that vibration become familiar. Memorize it. The more you feel relief, the more you actually feel good, the more accessible that feeling becomes even when things get rough.

And know that you are not alone. Ask for help when you need it—from friends and family, from the medical world, from your spiritual communities, and from the universe and life itself. Never underestimate your own strength. There is hope, and you have the ability to come through this.

Riding the Waves of Trauma

If you have a history of trauma, either physical or emotional, sometimes it will trigger and take you for a ride. Most of us have mild forms of these responses. When we get into arguments with people, our patterns come out to play. When we have a scare, or someone cuts us off in traffic, we react with a forceful energy that isn't warranted.

If you have deep trauma, the patterns can be intense and you might lose control. You may revert into a full-on temper tantrum, cycling through fear and rage and grief. You might say or do things that you wouldn't ordinarily say or do. These reactions feel extreme. The adrenaline and cortisol are pumping through your stronger-beating heart, and your breath becomes shallow and quick.

You may be able to observe yourself as the trauma reaction occurs. Other times, you are fully immersed in the cycle. Your awareness shuts off for a while, and adrenaline takes over. Some call it blind rage, but it can be blind fear or blind grief, too. Only when you calm down can you look back and see how your reaction was incongruous in relation to the trigger event. Afterward, your body may collapse from exhaustion or it may feel wired from the adrenaline. At this point, you need to find a way to regulate your system again.

Sometimes you can see the trigger starting to happen and prevent yourself from heading into the pattern. But if it's not caught soon enough, or if the catalyst continues to push the button, it won't be long before the instinctual part takes over. Once it's engaged, it requires time and focused energy to slow it down and reverse it. It's as if the roller coaster just got to the top of the climb, and when that first car starts down the hill, it's unstoppable.

We dislike being triggered so much that it's common to feel hatred for whomever or whatever triggered the alarm process. Even if you don't typically feel those feelings, the hatred comes when the instincts kick in. We have such a resistance to hatred that we often don't want to admit that we have it even though it's palpable in those moments. The longer you stay exposed to something that repeatedly pushes your buttons, the stronger the feeling will be, and evidence will build to support the notion that a particular person, place or thing is the cause of your suffering. Therefore, the hatred will seem well-placed and well-deserved.

The problem with that theory is that the feelings exist no matter who or what triggers them. In actuality, we hate our traumatic feelings. We hate feeling hate and fear and rage and grief and disgust. We hate that our instincts take over. In order to integrate that feeling into the array of emotions that we hold, it may be useful to see it as a simple reaction to fear and anger—an instinct that wants to obliterate the catalyst of our uncomfortable feelings.

Do you ever notice how important it becomes to be right when you are heated up in an argument? It can be over something that you don't care about at all. The stakes can be tiny, but you still have to be right. You can even see yourself needing to be right and know how ridiculous it is, but sometimes you can't stop it.

In these volatile moments, being wrong feels like we are exposing our jugular and rolling over, letting the threat win. Our instincts won't let that happen—so we fight for our lives, which in this case is being right.

How often do you look back and wonder why whatever you were defending was so important? How often do you avoid apologizing because it causes you to look at yourself when you were in a state of trauma, and you can't bear to admit that you said and did things you aren't proud of?

Be gentle with yourself as you're working through this extraordinarily difficult experience. Then, get better at practicing peace and tranquility. Get better at seeing what triggers you, admitting when it happens, and taking responsibility so you can cause the least amount of damage to yourself and others. And when you can't, that's okay, too. Work on forgiving yourself and know that you will get better at it as you continue to fine-tune your system and calibrate it toward happiness, peace and joy.

Perhaps you can turn those moments into a game. The game can be to look at the situation and your response through the lens of wonder, and notice how amazing and powerful the embodiment of your primal base emotions can be. Humbly bow to the magnificence of those feelings. Congratulate yourself for surviving. Instead of feeling disgust or shame, cultivate kindness and compassion for that amazing child you were who didn't know what to do in those moments, and realize that you did the best you could to cope.

Finally, be patient. Trauma takes as long as it takes to unravel. If you're lucky to be able to communicate with your partner or friends or family and tell them what you need when the trigger happens, that may help. But feeling your unsavory emotions is the key to freedom from them. And when it's all over, fill yourself up with love and gratitude. When you actually let those emotions flow and be felt, you free up so much inner space—let love fill it in.

Other Biological Considerations

Our biology cannot be discounted when we are talking about emotions and nervous system regulation. Sometimes there are powerful neurochemical influences at play.

Talk to the most centered 55-year-old woman you know, the one with years of meditation practice behind her, who seems to have it all together. Ask her if she had chemically-induced sleeplessness or anxiety as her hormones fluctuated. Ask the person with familial serotonin deficiencies if years of yoga and meditation were enough to counter their clinical depression. Ask someone with Addison's disease how they can quell their anxiety when their adrenal hormones are off. How about the cranky man with low testosterone?

I am a pretty sensitive being, and most medication or tweaking of my neurochemical balance can really set me off. When things are out of balance, interventions other than meditation are sometimes required to find the centered state where my feedback system is calibrated.

A healthy and balanced digestive and endocrine system are key to maximizing your feeling and intuitive instruments. When I am not in a hormonally balanced place, I can be a little more reactive instead of responsive. I may not be able to sleep as well, or I may feel a mild physical anxiety—even when I have no mental reason for it.

The techniques I offer help to bring you to your center or help process emotions. Learning to change the channel of your brain can be useful in fine-tuning your intuitive skills. What's cool about neurochemistry is that techniques like meditation actually *do* start to alter the chemistry. Often the things that help to improve your nervous system and reroute your pathways *do* change your hormone levels. But sometimes you may need to check for thyroid, adrenal, or male or female hormonal imbalances. You may also need to check your serotonin and dopamine levels and see if they need support.

The vast majority of neurochemicals are produced in your gut. So a healthy digestive system is essential to healthy hormonal balance. If you have chronic digestive issues, you can bet that your hormones will be off, and vice-versa. People are experiencing more digestive issues than ever before, and some of the chronic problems can be complicated to treat. We ingest all sorts of pesticides and biologically unrecognized substances that alter our gut biome balance. When our guts are out of balance, our whole health system is affected, including our neurochemistry.

The good news is that many highly intuitive people with tuned feeling systems also have gut imbalances and digestive issues. So it is still possible to trust your feelings even if your digestion isn't yet in balance.

It can be useful to consider consulting with an integrative doctor, a naturopath or Chinese or Ayurvedic practitioner to help bring balance to your system. The more vital you are, the clearer your feelings can be felt. When you have more energy available to you it increases the flow of life and your level of relaxation internally.

If you are a woman, prepare for your body to change. Menopause is usually a ten-year process, and hormones begin to fluctuate years before your periods stop. I would suggest getting a baseline hormonal test around 40 so that when you start having symptoms, you have a point of reference. Start planning action steps to support your body as your chemistry changes. And expect to rest a little more during this phase of your life.

Unlike it was for our ancestors, our fifties are a highly productive era of our lives, so while your body is going through a massive and chaotic change you are still asked to perform at the same level you did in your twenties. Respect that you may need to take a few more days off, pace yourself or take more naps as your body requires. This self-care doesn't make you old. You are learning to respect your body as it is working to find balance. And men, though it isn't spoken of as often, you can expect to have hormonal drops and changes as well.

Again, we are learning to hear our body's message and following that message the best we know how.

Calming the System Down

In order to get in touch with your inner signals and guidance, you first need to learn to relax out of fight-or-flight mode and into a calm and rested state of being. If you are someone who rarely feels relaxed, the chances are good that you are living in a perpetual low-grade state of fight-or-flight. If you are good at relaxing, then you likely only need to work on calming your system when something stressful happens that throws you out of balance. These suggested techniques are geared toward bringing you from the fight-or-flight state back into a more relaxed state.

When you start to address a hyper-stimulated nervous system, it's useful to actually honor the signals your system is giving you. When fear is firing in your body, the body's natural response is to retreat and curl up in a ball. This is the extreme posture of self-soothing, and is the physical posture our body wants to assume in order to calm down. More mild manifestations of this position can be slumping or bending forward, or looking down at the ground.

If you can arrange it, set a time and place to successfully relax. Find a quiet, dark room and set the mood with candles or light music. Only you know what helps you relax when it comes to your environment. Take the time to set up a safe place to perform these exercises.

Knowing that curling into a ball is the preferred natural reaction to fear, you may start in that position. Or if you prefer, child's pose in yoga is a re-creation of that posture. Allow yourself to breathe and feel your body in this posture. Allow your breath to soothe you and hold you. Allow any emotions to surface if they want to. Have the sense that you are giving yourself a hug.

Once you have brought yourself into the present moment, choose one of the techniques below and try it out. See if it resonates or makes you feel a little calmer, more relaxed and uplifted. Find one or two that work for you and make it a habit to gift yourself 10-15 minutes a day of self-nurturing.

There are many techniques and visualizations available for relaxation. If you know one that works for you, just make the commitment to use it. I've compiled a few that I have used at different times to help bring my nervous system back to center. If you tend to have a lot of stress or have suffered from trauma, I suggest making some of these techniques a part of your daily practice. Remember, the brain requires repetition to make lasting changes.

Rooting to the Earth

Because each of us is on an individual journey, every person I see presents differently. Even so, I do see common patterns. One of them, especially in individuals with trauma histories or who tend to be more sensitive by nature, is difficulty fully rooting their energy into the earth.

Though I cannot purport to know why this is, I can theorize. Because it can be difficult to live on this planet, and because it feels so nice to be in more of a meditative state, sensitive people may be afraid to feel what's happening in their bodies and on the earth. As a protective mechanism, they dissociate from their lower chakras and root, choosing instead to live in the ether. Unfortunately, instead of being safer, we actually become less stable and earth becomes a harder place to be.

When the sympathetic nervous system (fight-or-flight) gets activated, our energy shoots upwards, and we lose our grounded stability. There is much documentation and a pretty solid understanding physiologically as to why our digestive and reproductive systems shut down during stress, but also consider that the bulk of our energy is no longer in our first three chakras. How can those areas function optimally if we are too much in our heads and not inhabiting the areas that make our biology work properly? We will explore the chakras in depth later in this chapter.

When we get triggered into the fight-or-flight mode, our mind grabs onto the energy and continues to spin panicked tales about everything that has gone wrong, could go wrong, or most definitely will go wrong.

Though we know intuitively that it's good medicine to ground our energy, get out of our heads, quiet the mind and breathe deeply, it can be a powerful and habitual force that keeps us in our loop and prevents us from bringing our awareness back into the belly, legs and feet. Despite all my practice and knowledge about calming the nervous system and grounding into my body, I still often find myself not entirely centered. I need to regularly practice grounding, and I often need to have outside help to reconnect me to the lower part of my body (through myofascial release, body or energy work, yoga, or nature).

It also seems that as we are more attuned to our intuition, as we increase our sensitivity and clear out our channels for better energy flow, that our biological bodies need time to adjust to the changes that are happening. This adaptation process can feel foreign and scary to the body, and it will physiologically react as if it is in danger.

I have found that every time I stretch and grow and become clearer, I need to then nurture my body and be gentle with it to help soothe it back into the parasympathetic state. Many times I simply need to sleep and rest more, but other times I need to hold off on stronger physical activity, opting instead for more restorative and gentle practices. At these times, I also need to be diligent with practices that ground my energy into the earth.

(TECHNIQUE) Grounding to the Earth's Core

This technique is a variation on the previous basic grounding technique.

Sit or stand in a comfortable position. If you can, be outside with your feet on the earth. Otherwise picture yourself somewhere in lush nature, such as a forest or by a lake or the beach. Slow your mind and bring awareness to your breath. Feel the parts of your body that are in contact with the earth. Feel the support underneath you.

Now visualize your feet, legs, and root (base of the spine) filling with a golden light. See that light extending to the ground and going deep down to the center core of the earth. See that golden strand wrap around and connect firmly with the earth's core. Feel the stable power of the earth's energy draw up the golden cord and into your legs and pelvis. Feel that energy fill your entire body. As the energy comes up into your body, notice how it helps stabilize and snug you into the ground. You are strong and supported. You can relax even deeper.

Know that you can quickly return to this grounded and centered state at any moment, simply by feeling that connection in your feet, legs and pelvis.

Grounding Self-Massage

A really simple way to bring your awareness back into your body and especially your low belly, legs and feet, is through gentle self-massage.

Touch helps to bring awareness to an area, and massage increases blood and energy flow.

When we get anxious or tense, our energy tends to get held above the diaphragm, and we lose contact with the lower part of the body, and along with it the feeling of stability and grounding. Our breath, as well as our sensation, leaves the area.

You can do this simple technique anytime during the day and for as long as you want or need to. You can opt to use oil or lotion, or you can just as easily massage over your clothes. In Ayurvedic medicine, sesame oil is suggested to help ground scattered energy.

A full-body self-massage is also a great idea, but I'm going to focus on the lower body here, so you have a good way to help ground quickly if needed.

(TECHNIQUE) **Self-Massage**

Start by relaxing and noticing your breath. Take a few breaths to feel into your belly, pelvis and legs. Notice your breath as it is right now. Use this as your baseline.

Beginning below the ribs in the upper abdomen/solar plexus area, make small, gentle circles in the center of the belly. Do this for a few moments, feeling the tension soften. Now place your hands on your ribs and use your fingers to gently sweep laterally (outward) beneath the ribs in the upper abdomen. Move your hands down to belly button height and laterally sweep here a few times. Then move into the low belly/pelvis with your hands on your hips and sweep across the low belly. Take a few more deep breaths, feeling the ease and expansion you created in your belly.

Now make loose fists with your hands and gently drum along your sacrum and gluteal muscles, as well as out toward the sides of the hips. Spend some extra time on the sacrum, as this area tends to hold a lot of tension. Allow the drumming to head up toward the low back and kidney areas as well. Be gentle. If you like, you can use your thumbs to laterally sweep across the low back and buttocks in the same way that you did with the abdomen. Take a few more deep breaths.

Starting with the left leg, use both hands to massage the upper part of the hip, down to the knee. Use kneading motions, and spend all the time you need tending to any sore or numb areas. Get the front, sides and back of the thigh. Then begin doing some long strokes from the top of the hip down to the knee, and back up. Again, address the front, back and sides of your thighs. Now make circular motions around the inner and outer knee joint. Move into kneading motions down the front and back of the calf and shin, followed by long stroking motions up and down the calf, from the knee to the ankle and back up. Now circle around the front and back of the ankle and massage around the bones on the sides. Do a couple of gentle pinches to the Achilles, and then use your hands to move the ankle in circles clockwise and counterclockwise.

Gently stroke up and down the arch of the foot and massage across the arch from side to side. Massage each toe, and up and down the top of the foot from each toe to the ankle. Gently pause and breathe, feeling the vitality and sensation in your left leg. When you are ready, follow the same procedure with the right leg.

Restorative Yoga

Finding a good in-person or online restorative yoga class is highly recommended to help calm the nervous system. Restorative yoga involves supported reclined postures that are held for five minutes or longer and are particularly designed to settle the nervous system and promote deep rest. Most communities have a restorative yoga class somewhere. If you can't find a class, there are several written and online sources of the poses. Choose a couple of postures at the end of each day to help soothe your system.

Sound as Healer

The ancient holy texts make reference to sound preceding form. The Gospel of John opens with, "In the beginning was the word, and the word was with God and the word was God." And in Hinduism, OM is referenced several times throughout the Upanishads as being the representation of Brahma (the all/God). They speak of a primordial sound or vibration that became all that is.

Sound is an amazing tool that we have at our disposal. Studies have shown that sound torture is the worst type of torture, and conversely that music or pleasant sound can raise you into a state of bliss. I use my voice and sound regularly to create a rapid and powerful change within.

Scientifically speaking, singing and humming help to stimulate the vagus nerve, which is a doorway to peace and relaxation. Listening to music or chanting, or birds or water or nature creates a calming effect as well, but I highly suggest using your own voice and vibration if you want a fast track to feeling better.

You can be as devotional or as playful as you want to be when it comes to singing. If you doubt that singing makes you feel better, try turning on your favorite song to sing along with and see how you feel afterward. Because I have seen the power of words and thoughts in creating my own vibratory state, I suggest that you choose to sing something that you love and that increases your vibration into an expanded and joyful state. The association you have with a song will play a part in the feelings you create.

I often use sound as a quick way to tune-up the instrument of my physical body. I like to change it up, so I don't always sing the same thing. I love the Sanskrit mantras, and I often go through phases where I sing along with kirtan music or chants. I also have practiced *japa*, which involves reciting a mantra 108 times. If I have less time, I'll do fewer repetitions, perhaps 9 or 27, and sometimes I don't even keep track of how many times I repeat the mantra; I simply repeat until I feel better.

Setting Intention

The word mantra means mind protection. When using a mantra, setting an intention and summoning the vibration of that intention during your practice can significantly increase the benefits. Sing it like you mean it!

For example, if you choose to do a Ganesh mantra, and you know that Ganesh is thought to be the remover of obstacles, you may set an intention that obstacles to joy, peace, harmony and happiness are removed as you sing. As you set this intention, create the feeling of joy, peace and harmony. Feel the walls and barriers to the joyful feeling fall away, as joy and peace expand and increase.

Another good way to use mantras is to sing directly to your chakras. This is the method that I use the most often, and it is the technique I will give in full. It is thought that the sounds and syllables of the Sanskrit language are healing to the body. Sanskrit has many seed (*Bija*) syllables, which correlate to a variety of things including the planets and the elements. It can be used intentionally to help open and heal the part of us that correlates with a particular sound.

Chakras: Wheels of Life

Many people are familiar with the Sanskrit term chakra, which translates into wheel. The use of the word in respect to the body describes areas of energetic churning. These areas are powerful vortex sites within our bodies that are thought to be access points to universal energy. Each of these vortices has a specific correlation and association that is generally accepted. Several sources speak of many chakra systems, varying from three to eighteen, depending on the source. I will discuss the most common Western model of the chakras and their associations based on people's experiences. I encourage you to meditate or feel into your own energy centers and trust what you see or experience as more truthful than anything you read about or that I suggest here. Because this model is commonly accepted, I offer it as a starting point to help access and feel these parts of yourself. I am also offering a few thoughts from my personal experience with these chakras that might resonate.

The chakra vortices energetically reach both the front and the back of your body, or in the case of the root and crown, extend downward and up, respectively. You may see or experience them like a conical swirl of energy, similar to how water looks as it flows down a drain, or you may feel a pulsation or aliveness that is stronger than in other areas.

I experience the chakras three-dimensionally in and outside/around my body as spheres of energy, not simply as the two-dimensional representations we see on paper. As you are noticing your own energy centers, feel in all directions so you can determine if there are weaker spots and places that are more easily noticed.

Muladhara—Root, First Chakra

The first chakra resides at the base of the spine, near the tailbone and perineum. This chakra tends to be associated with the earth element and our grounding stability on the planet. This is the region associated with safety and basic needs. A strong root chakra brings energy into our legs and feet, connects us to the earth, and helps us to feel grounded and stable.

The body parts most often affected by the first chakra are hips, legs, feet, low back, bones and joints.

The color generally associated with this area is red, and the *Bija* sound is that of the earth element: LAM. (Each seed sound rhymes with "HUM.")

Svadhisthana—Sacral, Second Chakra

The second chakra is said to reside near the sacrum and low belly/pelvis. This chakra is associated with our sexuality, our creative life force, and our family/tribal connection. A healthy second chakra feels alive and creative, has a healthy and balanced relationship with sexuality and connection and helps us feel secure in our relationships. This is the area of our sensuality.

The areas of the body affected by this chakra are generally the hips and low back, pelvic and reproductive organs, and bowels.

The color associated with this chakra is orange, its element is water, and the *Bija* mantra of water is VAM.

Manipura—Solar Plexus, Third Chakra

In the area of the solar plexus, right under the rib cage and extending back to the T-12 area between the kidneys, lies the third chakra. This area is associated with personal power and will, as well as assimilation and digestion—both physically and energetically. The development of this chakra is linked to healthy self-esteem and the presentation of the self in the world, as well as empathy and ability to feel what is happening energetically around us.

This chakra is associated with our digestive organs including liver, stomach/spleen, pancreas, kidneys, mid and lower back, and ribs.

The element is fire, the color is yellow, and the *Bija* mantra for fire is RAM.

Anahata—Heart, Fourth Chakra

In the center of the chest, from sternum to the mid-scapula area, sits the fourth chakra. This area is generally regarded as the connection point between the physical chakras below and the esoteric universal chakras above. This is also the point associated with love and connection. Of all the chakras, this one probably gets the most attention in yoga classes, and with good reason. "Open your heart" or "heart-centered" are phrases often used in regular language to illustrate the importance of this area.

A healthy heart chakra reflects the qualities of love, compassion, joy, kindness and connection. When this chakra is open and strong, we feel expanded and loving, radiating with happiness.

The body parts associated with this chakra are the heart and lungs, breasts, rib cage, scapula, shoulders and arms.

The element is wind, the colors associated with this area are pink and green, and the *Bija* mantra for wind is YAM.

Vishuddha—Throat, Fifth Chakra

The throat chakra resides from the C7 vertebra at the base of the neck to the front of the throat. This area is associated with expression, clarity and truth. It is the region that connects the heart to the head and is the vehicle for relating with the outside world through communication. A healthy and well-developed throat chakra allows for clarity and truth to come out of your mouth, a skilled ability to listen and an authentic expression of your heart's desires.

The body parts associated with this area are the neck and throat, thyroid, jaw, mouth and tongue. Swallowing our truth can adversely affect the solar plexus as well, as the esophagus joins those areas together.

The color of the throat chakra is blue, the element is space/ether, and the *Bija* sound is HAM.

Ajna—Third Eye, Sixth Chakra

From the base of the skull to the center of the forehead, encompassing our pineal and pituitary glands is the sixth chakra. This area is associated with wisdom and thought as well as higher intuition and perception. Besides the heart chakra, this is the other chakra that has received significant attention in spiritual circles, as it connects us to seeing beyond the physical plane of existence. This is the region people refer to as the third eye. And because of its association with the mind, focusing here can quickly quiet the mind.

A well-developed sixth chakra allows for a high level of intuitive wisdom and clear thinking, even to the point of psychic abilities.

The body parts associated with this area are the pituitary and pineal glands, the brain, head, mouth and jaw.

The color is indigo, this area is considered beyond elements, and the *Bija* mantra is OM (pronounced OHM).

Sahasrara—Crown, Seventh Chakra

The seventh or crown chakra lies above the top of the head in the auric field. This chakra is the connection to source. A well-developed crown chakra will create spiritual connectedness and higher knowing and integration with your divine nature.

The areas associated with this chakra are the head and nervous system, and imbalances can manifest as energetic experiences such as agitation, as well as skin rashes or headaches. In severe cases, delusions and mental illness can occur. In my own experience, these dysfunctions tend to happen when the crown is active, but the energy hasn't been fully grounded into the rest of the system. An open and integrated crown chakra occurs during deep meditation.

The colors associated with the crown chakra are violet, purple and white, and the *Bija* mantra is SO-HUM. (I have also seen AUM or "silent OM" cited as the *Bija* for this area.)

Chakra	Location	Color	Element	Main Attributes	Bija Sound	Affirmation
Muladhara Root Chakra	Tailbone	Red	Earth	Strength Stability Safety	LAM	"I am safe and supported on the earth"
Svadhistana Sacral Chakra	Sacrum and Low Belly/ Pelvis	Orange	Water	Creativity Sexuality Tribal/Family Connection	VAM	"I am connected to my sensual vitality and creative life force"
Manipura Solar Plexus	Diaphragm T-11/12 and upper belly	Yellow	Fire	Personal power Strength Will	RAM	"I am powerful. I assimilate life with ease and grace"
Anahata Heart Chakra	Center of the upper back to chest/sternum	Green Pink	Air	Love of self and others Compassion	YAM	"I am love"
Visshudha Throat	Base of the neck to the throat	Blue	Ether	Speaking truth Connecting head to heart Creative expression	HAM	"I communicate clearly and speak my truth"
Ajna Third Eye	Base of the skull to center of the brow	Indigo	Beyond Elements	Higher thought Intuition Psychic seeing	OM	"I am intuitive and wise"
Sahashara Crown Chakra	Above the head	Violet White	Beyond Elements	Wisdom Connection to higher source	(OHM) SO-HAM	"I am spiritually connected to all that is"

TECHNIQUE ## Singing to the Chakras

I encourage you to begin this technique in a quiet place where you can really feel the resonance of the practice, but I often use these syllables during regular activities, for instance while in the car on my way to work to tune my body for the day. Below is the longer, more complete version of this exercise, but feel free to just sing the syllable that you feel you need and you will get many of the benefits.

Get comfortable and relaxed. Bring your awareness to the base of your spine/perineum and tailbone area. Picture a red glowing light. Create the intention, "I am safe and supported on the earth" either aloud or in your mind. Cultivate the feeling of that intention. As you become aware of that area, take a deep breath. Exhale with the sound of LAM, directing the sound into the red light, feeling the stability increase as you make the sound. Repeat the sound three times.

Now bring your awareness up to the second chakra, sacrum and low belly/pelvis. Picture an orange light and feel the watery fluidity of this area. Create the intention: "I am connected to my sensual vitality and creative life force." Feel the vibration of creativity and sensuality fill up this orange light as you inhale. Exhale with VAM, maintaining that feeling. Repeat two more times.

Bring your awareness to the area of your solar plexus and kidneys. Visualize a yellow light and the element of fire. Create the intention: "I am powerful. I assimilate life with ease and grace." Feel the vibration of power and ease simultaneously fill this area. Inhale deeply, and exhale RAM. Repeat this two more times.

Move your awareness up into the center of your chest and picture a vibrant green light. Infuse the light with the intention, "I am love." Feel the feeling of gratitude, love, and compassion fill up this area as you inhale. Exhale YAM. Repeat two more times.

Next move into the center of your throat and picture a blue sphere of light. Cultivate the feeling of clarity and truth and create the intention: "I communicate clearly and speak my truth." Inhale, then exhale HAM. Repeat three times.

Bring your awareness to the center of your head and brow. Picture an indigo sphere of light and infuse that area with the feelings of stillness and wisdom. Create the intention, "I am intuitive and wise." Inhale deeply and exhale OM into that indigo light. Repeat two more times.

Move your awareness to above the crown of your head and visualize a violet sphere of light. Feel your scalp relax and open into this chakra. Cultivate a feeling of unity with your true divinity, or God if you prefer. Create the intention, "I am spiritually connected to all that is (or God)." Inhale deeply and exhale, SO-HUM. Repeat three times.

Close your eyes and feel your whole system vibrating with the intentions you have created. Notice the quiet, expansive relaxation of your mind.

Chinese Organ Breath Sounds * 🎧

In the Qigong tradition, there are five elements associated with the five organ systems of the body, as well as a sixth energetic meridian associated with the nervous system. Chinese medicine is pretty complex, so even if I knew it inside and out, explaining it in any depth would be impossible in the context of this work. The sounds that we use are meant to create a vibration in the body that helps to move stagnant qi/chi (energy) from different areas of the body.

The "organs" in Chinese medicine aren't actual organs but instead have specific energetic functions. And each organ that we address with the sounds has a paired organ, as well. When the sound is addressing the liver, for example, it also affects its paired organ, the gallbladder. There is a sixth energetic organ in Chinese medicine called the triple warmer that can confuse Westerners since it doesn't have an anatomical counterpart. This "organ" helps regulate the fluids and energy in the spaces of the body and it pairs with the pericardium. The Chinese system does not have a one-to-one relationship with the physical organs, so because you may have liver qi/chi stagnation, it does not necessarily translate to having a problem with your actual liver. But in my experience, I do feel the general areas of the organs resonate and vibrate as I make the various sounds.

Different Chinese Qigong systems utilize different breath sounds; some are louder and some are aspirate (whispered). I am sharing the method that I learned from my first yoga teacher, who taught a Taoist form of yoga, and these sounds are done in a whisper.

When I practice these, I usually repeat each sound three times. You can opt to rotate through all six sounds and repeat the complete cycle three times. I usually prefer to repeat each sound three times so that I can feel (and taste) the movement of the chi from each area along with the immediate results of these simple, but powerful sounds. If I'm feeling a little congested or achy in one area, I will sometimes only do the corresponding sound, or spend more time with that area than with the others. If I am experiencing the emotion that correlates to one particular organ, I will focus on that area.

If you are a visual person, you can picture light filling up each area as you inhale and then picture a muddy light releasing as you exhale. Imagine the breath is collecting any stagnant chi and bringing it out of the body with your exhale. I will list the correlating elements and colors along with the sounds below.

Organ	Paired Organ	Element	Color	Emotion (imbalanced)	Emotion (balanced)	Sound (whispered)
Liver	Gallbladder	Metal	Green	Anger	Patience	SHHHH
Heart	Small Intestine	Fire	Red	Despair/ Hate	Love/Joy	HAAAA
Spleen	Stomach	Earth	Yellow	Worry/ Overthinking	Empathy	HOOOO
Kidneys	Bladder	Water	Blue	Fear	Courage	SHOOOO
Lungs	Large Intestine	Air	Gray	Sadness/ Grief	Composure	SSSSS
Triple Warmer	Pericardium	Fire	Red	Despair/ Hate	Nervous System Balance	HEEEE

The Power of Smell

The limbic system of your brain is an area that can store trauma and deep emotion. It is also the place that houses old memories. Because it is situated right next to the olfactory center of the brain, the sense of smell can be a direct path toward relaxing (or agitating) the limbic system.

This is one reason why people who are stuck in fight-or-flight, those with PTSD, chronic trauma or who are in the throes of a migraine, tend to be strongly affected by smell, and often in a negative way.

Because we have this doorway directly into the brain, capitalizing on pleasant smells can be quickly relaxing, expansive and euphoric.

Smell is a highly individual experience, and people have specific associations with what they like and don't like. I know plenty of people who love the smell of permanent markers or gasoline and others who loathe the smell of lavender and rose.

The "dose" of the smell also varies by person. For example, I can't handle any sort of synthetic smell that maintains a pungent aroma for a long period of time. Perfumes and lotions with synthetic fragrance or room fresheners drive me mad, but I know other people who don't get bothered by, and actually enjoy, those long-lasting fragrances.

The most recent research is showing that synthetic fragrance is actually harmful to our bodies. Many of them contain chemicals, including benzene derivatives, aldehydes, phthalates, and a slew of other known toxins that are capable of causing cancer, congenital disabilities, nervous-system disorders and allergies. If you are unsure if your products contain these chemicals, they are listed on the label. A good rule of thumb is if you see the word "fragrance" on a product, even if it's "natural fragrance," it probably contains at least one of those chemicals.

Several years ago, I worked with an excellent neurologist who specializes in migraine headaches. He wisely pointed out that the sensitive people of the world are the ones who likely help keep us from harm. They are the canaries in the coalmine as they react more quickly to adverse substances than people who are less sensitive. They help expose things that aren't good for us.

That said, you know yourself best, and if your vanilla lotion brings you great joy and soothes you, then you can choose to use it.

My first and favorite suggestion for adding soothing scents into your world is through essential oils. The oils are the most concentrated form of scent in plant materials. Some oils are quite inexpensive, while others are costly. Usually, the cost is determined by how much plant material is required to extract the oil, how rare it is, or how long the material has to grow before it is harvested. For example, citrus oils express a very large amount of oil with a small amount of plant material, so they tend to be relatively inexpensive. Some of the floral oils require large quantities of petals or plant material to yield a tiny amount of oil. Rose oil, for example, requires fifty pounds of petals to create one milliliter of oil. Frankincense is a tree that grows only in a very small region of the world, and it must be quite mature before oils can be extracted from it. Sandalwood has to be fifty years old before oils can be harvested. These oils are therefore costly.

Essential oils are also the immune system of the plant, so they all possess antimicrobial properties. Some are better suited to fighting certain types of microbes than others, but they all have positive health benefits. We can get many of the benefits—psychologically and physically—from inhaling the oils, so using a non-heated diffuser or a humidifier that is built to handle essential oils can create the effects you desire.

Many of the oils can be applied topically in a diluted state as well. I generally dilute my oils with jojoba oil, since it tends to be closest to our natural skin oil pH, but people use all sorts of carrier oils, including olive or grapeseed oil.

Some of the oils can be irritating to the skin, so those *must* be diluted. I usually just avoid using them outside of diffusion. Others, such as lavender, are gentle and safe and don't need such a strong dilution.

As a rule of thumb, I do not recommend ingesting essential oils. I know there is some controversy around this, as many of the oils have medicinal benefits. But unless you are explicitly trained in dosing with the oils, it's just not a good idea to mess with such strong medicine. Remember, the oils are potent. They are the most reduced part of the immune system of the plant, so the effects are considerable. We have a delicate balance of microbes in our gut, and ingesting strong medicine like that can create an imbalance, much like taking antibiotics does.

Essential oils are easy to find, and you can select a scent that resonates with you. You can also play with the many blends that seasoned aromatherapists have created. My personal blends tend toward psycho-spiritual well-being through the scent, but many also impart more therapeutic effects. Whatever you choose, simply add five or six drops of the oil (or oils) to your diffuser and allow the magic to unfold.

(TECHNIQUE) Direct Oil Application

If you prefer to use the oil more directly, dilute it with a carrier oil and put a few drops into your palm. Rub your hands together and take a few long inhalations, breathing the scent deep into your body. Feel your body relax with the exhalation.

Place the oil on a body part that could use a bit more energy. The heart, the back of the neck or the solar plexus are some good choices. You can also rub the oil into your feet, which is especially useful for grounding.

Once you've applied the oil, hold your palm over the area to allow the oil to saturate your skin. (Essential oils evaporate quickly, so it's useful to keep your hand there for a good minute or so.)

Return your hands to your nose and take a few more breaths, allowing yourself to enjoy the scent and feel the effects penetrate deeply into your body.

6

When the Going Gets Tough
Practicing When it's Hard to Practice

Sometimes life feels chaotic. There may be many unknowns or things up in the air. You may be facing a disease or massive loss. Or maybe something inside of you is creating chaos because the old way of being just isn't working anymore.

Chaos can feel scary and unsettling. It can create anxiety and unease and grief and frustration. Life seems as if it's swirling and blowing debris all around. When we are in chaos, our instincts become fired up and we hold on with white knuckles, pleading for things to stay the same.

The energy of chaos is the power of transformation. When you look to myths and stories throughout the ages, they echo the truth of reality on this planet. If you watch the cycles of nature, the same is reflected. Things die and fall away to allow new growth to happen. Destruction precedes creation. We aren't always conscious of the need for loss as it is occurring. In fact, we tend to resist it with every ounce of energy we can muster, even if we have been working toward creating something new and we know we need to let go of the thing that is being destroyed or dying away.

When the storms stir up and unsettle us, it is easy to let the anxiet-ies of the mind take over, and we may start thinking we have to get to work on solving problems related to this upset. Sometimes action is required, but more often our worry far exceeds anything we can do. The mind spins with scenarios that grab hold of us, keeping us from resting in the calm and creative state of being that allows real informa-tion to flow through.

When we're faced with chaos, we convince ourselves we have too much to do, so we cannot practice the very things that help us be more effective during these times. There is a saying, "Meditate for twenty minutes every day, unless you are busy—then meditate for an hour."

I am the first person to admit that when I get stressed and busy, and life is requiring a lot of me, I often skip my yoga, shorten my meditations (or skip them entirely), believing that I just have too much to do. Or my mind is so active that I know calming it is a big ask, so I'd rather not sit still knowing that my fifteen minutes may only give me two minutes of relative meditation. Even with all of the experiences I've had, I somehow *still* have times where I let my mind talk me out of the things I know will help me.

When I'm in a more agitated state of mind, and I've been thrown from my center, I often have to do something active rather than sitting still. Some people are gifted at sitting, dropping into the meditative space and waiting for the waves to calm. I can sometimes do that, too. There are excellent tools for achieving stillness when stillness seems far away.

The easiest one is focused, active exercise. My top choice is yoga. It is a tried-and-true ally and is designed to bring the mind, the breath and the body together. Even when I "don't have time" to do yoga, I find that doing a few sun salutations and a standing posture or two is just what I need to still myself enough to sit for a few minutes.

I can't argue myself out of ten minutes of yoga and five minutes of meditation. That's one snooze button less of sleep, one less email returned. We all have fifteen minutes somewhere in our day; we've just become savvy at convincing ourselves that other things are more essential. This is especially true when we are in the midst of change and chaos.

Using Your Breath

I have already discussed some basic breath techniques to practice feeling into your body. This tool can also be utilized in a more mentally focused way to help calm an agitated system.

The breath gives the mind something to focus on that is body-centric, and you are accessing and paying attention to your life force as it comes in and out of your body. One note of caution about breathwork: Because our bodies are used to maintaining a certain balance of oxygen and carbon dioxide, you can occasionally feel agitated when you start to manipulate the breath. Anytime you start feeling stress in the body while doing breathwork, let go of the breath technique for a few rounds, and begin again once your system rebalances. The more you do breathwork, the less this tends to happen.

I have two favorite mind-calming breath patterns that I use on a regular basis: *nadi shodhana* and a technique for increasing your exhalation.

Nadi Shodhana: Alternate Nostril Breathing

The first technique is a *kriya* called *nadi shodhana*, or alternate nostril breathing. This breath requires focus since you are changing the pattern of breath flow by blocking a nostril as you breathe in and out. It's complex enough that it tethers the mind quite nicely and pretty quickly.

Energetically, it is said that *nadi shodhana* is useful for balancing the two sides of the body/brain. In the yogic energetic model, the central channel goes up and down through the spine. (Think of your spinal cord as a physical visual of this channel.) The yogis say that when this channel is open we are centered, and connected to the source. There are two other main channels on each side of this central channel. They are said to either meet or intersect at each of our chakras as they travel up along the spine and central channel. The theory is that both these channels must be open and balanced in order for energy to flow more effectively through the central channel.

The left nostril correlates to the lunar, restful energies or, in scientific terms, to the parasympathetic nervous system. The right nostril correlates to the solar and active energies, or the sympathetic nervous system.

Alternate nostril breathing focuses breath into one of these side channels followed by the other (alternating between them). As you practice, this alternating breath brings more energetic balance to your body and nervous system.

(TECHNIQUE) *Nadi Shodhana*

Sit or lie in a comfortable position with your spine straight. If you choose to sit, it's okay to support the spine with something behind your back. Whether upright or reclined, this technique is best achieved with a fairly straight spine to maximize the flow of energy through the central channel.

Slow your breath and close your eyes. Traditionally, *nadi shodhana* is taught using the right hand with the index and middle finger bent down toward the palm, and the fourth and fifth fingers straight (and if you're able, the fourth finger crossed over the pinky). Some practitioners will opt instead to put the index and middle finger at the point of the third eye, between the eyebrows. The thumb will be used to block the right nostril, and the fourth finger will block the left nostril. If this is a hard position for you to grasp, it's also okay to just use alternating thumbs to block your nostrils, or even just to imagine you are blocking each side with your mind.

Place your thumb over the right nostril and inhale through the left. Then close the left nostril, exhaling through the right. Inhale through the right, close the right, and exhale through the left. Inhale left, then close the left and exhale right. Continue this pattern of breathing for a few rounds, maybe six to ten cycles or longer if it feels right. On the final round, after you exhale through the left nostril, release both nostrils and take a few breaths noticing how your mind and body feel. Transition to meditation if this seems right for you.

(TECHNIQUE) ## Increasing the Exhale

Another very effective way to use the breath to center and calm the mind is a simple technique that tethers your mind to a count of your breath.

I love doing this technique lying with my legs up the wall, or with my knees bent and shins on a chair or couch so that my psoas and belly can be free and relaxed. You can also just lie on your back or sit up for this technique.

Energetically and physiologically, the exhalation corresponds to letting go, relaxing, calming. It's the moon energy, which tends to ground the body and mind. The inhalation is more stimulating and energizing. So by increasing the exhalation, we are bringing ourselves into a calmer state.

Start by getting comfortable, and pay attention to your natural breath. Try to just observe it without thinking it needs to be any different than it is. Begin here. Notice what your body intelligence has created to regulate your oxygen and carbon dioxide balance. Cultivate gratitude that your breath knows exactly how to keep you in balance.

Now, notice how long your natural inhalation is by adding a count to it. Then count how long your exhalation naturally is. Notice this for a few rounds of breath.

Then gently intend for the inhale and exhale counts to be even. If your natural inhale takes four counts, allow your exhale to match it at four counts. See how your body feels as you breathe with equal inhales and exhales. Remember, if you start to feel agitated at all or like you are putting a lot of effort into the technique, drop it and allow your body to do what comes naturally for a few breaths. When you feel ready, you can begin again.

Once you have taken a few rounds of breath with equal inhale and exhale counts, try to extend the exhale by one count, so that you are exhaling slightly longer than inhaling. Continue this pattern for several rounds. Then release the technique and notice your state of being.

Using a Mantra

Another effective way of helping to calm an agitated mind is by using a mantra. Mantra means, "mind protection." Many cultures use this technique, though the yoga and Hindu traditions have made it the most famous.

When you do mantra practice, you repeat a particular word, sound or phrase over and over. This process gives the mind a task and helps to keep it focused. Some traditions believe that certain sounds create a distinct change in your brain and your being. Sanskrit is structured so that every sound and syllable creates an effect, so it tends to use mantras quite frequently. Transcendental Meditation (TM) is a specific type of meditation that gives you a mantra to use as your personal doorway to stillness.

The Catholic Church is another example of the use of mantras. Praying the rosary, for instance, is repeating phrases/prayers with energetic meaning behind them. Reciting the "Hail Mary" and "Our Father" prayers over and over creates a sense of calm and connection in the brain.

Because I have seen the power of mantra in my own life, I highly suggest this technique for anyone and everyone. You don't need to have any religious or spiritual inclination in order for it to work. Any phrase or set of syllables will do the trick, but I suggest choosing something that brings up positive feelings as you say it. Some ideas outside of the traditional Sanskrit phrases (which are easily found online—there's a mantra for almost everything) are "I am love," "I am peace," "I am joy." Anything that rings true or resonates for you is a good choice.

(TECHNIQUE) **Using a Mantra**

There are two ways to approach mantra use. The first is to recite it over and over in your mind (or audibly if possible). You can use a mala (Buddhist prayer beads) or a rosary (Catholic prayer beads) to count how many times you say the phrase. You can count on your knuckles or you can just set a timer and use the mantra for a set period. There are structured practices in different traditions as far as how many times to say mantras, but it's also okay to use it in whatever way resonates the most for you.

The second way to use a mantra is to coordinate it with your breath. This is a slower, more focused and deliberate use of the mantra. For example, if your mantra is "I am love" ("*Aha prema*" in Sanskrit), you can inhale "I am," and exhale "love." (Inhale "*Aha*" and exhale "*prema.*")

Both methods work but have slightly different approaches and effects. I use each method at different times. Try each to see which works best for you. After you finish your several-minute mantra practice, again, breathe and notice how you feel.

Trusting the Universe

Calming the nervous system requires that you surrender the control you think you have over every aspect of your life. This may seem obvious, or it may seem like you already have surrendered (you don't think you are trying to control things anymore). You may have come so far that you don't recognize the subtle ways that you are still putting your hands on the wheel of your life and trying to steer it in a direction that may or may not be congruent with the way that life is flowing.

Our lives are completely held and completely supported. Simply step back and look at how the planet is spinning, and the earth and moon are revolving, how gravity is holding us in place, how the flowers and trees are blooming and shedding and sprouting from seeds. Babies are born and people age and die. All that occurs on this planet happens without us being consciously involved. Our cuts heal without us thinking about it, our bodies breathe and our hearts beat without us controlling them.

If all of these miraculous things are happening every moment of every day, then we cannot deny that there is a greater force at work than our own will. Yet, it's quite easy to think that on some level we have a say. It's common to think that if we act in certain ways, the world will bend to our desire and that we can have a major impact on the flow of life. Finding the humility in this realization (or reminder) can be a little bit scary, but it can also be a massive relief. Imagine for a moment that everything is completely taken care of. Imagine that the details of your life are handled and all you need to do is rest in the comforting arms of the force that is taking care of it all.

I'm not implying that you don't have to do anything. But what if the actions you do take feel inspired and directed, instead of wound-up, tight and frantic and holding so much importance?

My work can cause me to feel responsible for the clients on my table. It's easy to think that what I do in the moments they are in my room, and what I send them home to work on, is going to make or break their healing process. It's actually been quite a difficult path for me to remove the feelings of responsibility from my practice. It's hard for me to not over-effort, or to detach from the outcome of the client in front of me. It can be hard to admit to myself that I have only a small offering to give, and that the fate of their path is not within my control.

Luckily, I have a highly sensitive body system that alerts me to the moments (or sometimes whole seasons) when I have forgotten that I am simply showing up and offering inspired ideas and action to assist my clients in their journeys. I can forget that we are both held by this greater force, and that their soul is directing the trajectory of their own life and healing. Sometimes I start to feel tired, drained and dull instead of centered, inspired and full of life. Even when I know the truth, even when I practice centering, there are times when my need to control overrides these truths. It's subtle, and occasionally I miss it. But when you have a history of thinking that your actions are essential to fixing and changing things that already have a life of their own, those subtle energies can still present themselves.

Trusting the universe is harder than it seems. It's a total surrender to the idea that there is very little you can do, and believing that things are really okay exactly as they are. It's trusting that even if we don't put in much effort, things will work out in a beautiful way. And that if things don't seem to work out so beautifully, that is okay, too.

(TECHNIQUE)   Let Yourself Be Held

Lie on your side, in a fetal position. Feel as if someone has his or her arms around you, letting you know that everything is okay. Let yourself feel the sense of soothing parental support, as if this figure is taking away all your worries. If it is helpful, you can have a loved one actually put their arms around you in this way. Allow your body to relax layer by layer as you melt into this embrace. Feel in this moment what it is like to trust that all is well, and know that you don't need to do anything to make it so. Let yourself release your tension and your need to take action, and surrender to the calm, steady support around you. Feel it all melt away. Let all your cells absorb this sensation.

Tell yourself that you are held, you are safe and you are loved. Go beyond what your mind may tell you, and allow yourself to accept and surrender to this truth. Feel yourself breathing. Feel your heart beating. Connect to the force that allows these things to happen. Allow yourself to sink into the bed and melt into the energetic arms around you. Maybe even give yourself a hug. Let yourself be soothed.

Your Body Talks

We may not believe that we have all the answers at our disposal. We may not have learned to trust ourselves fully. And why should we? We have most likely spent years conditioning ourselves to override our instincts. We have strengthened the pathways of logic and reason, or worse, the pathway of fear.

We abandon the truth that our body tries to communicate to us. We feel our bodies get tired, but we have that extra cup of coffee to push through instead of resting. We get those low back twinges whenever we sit at our computer for too long, but we keep on working. Our skin breaks out and our joints ache when we eat a lot of sugar, but we put up with it and keep eating quick, easy snacks instead of nourishing meals.

Your body is always giving you signals, and the signs are usually rather subtle like a tap on the shoulder at first. But when you continue to ignore the gentle cues, the body gets louder and louder. One day you'll get sick and be forced to rest. Or you'll move the wrong way and your back will spasm to the point of not being able to sit or walk. Or your skin flare-ups and joint aches will become arthritis or digestion problems.

Emotionally, your body gives you similar messages. Maybe you had a bad feeling about getting into business with a certain person, but you shook it off and ignored it. Perhaps you took the job that was a safe bet, even though your heart told you the other one would make you happy.

You knew that you should have said no to your friend when she asked you for help, but you did it out of obligation.

When you make decisions, everything else suddenly carries more weight than your feelings. But your inner knowing is right. Check into your own life and see if it's true for you. Look at how many times you have said to yourself, "I knew better," or "If only I'd listened to my gut."

Get better at listening to the cues your body gives you. That stomachache you always get after you have pizza? It's telling you something. I'm not suggesting that you have to avoid experiences based on your feelings or associations, but at least acknowledge that you have heard your body. If you know pizza makes you feel bad, start making conscious choices about it. Occasionally, it might be worth it to enjoy the flavor of pizza. But understand that your body is telling you that it isn't resonating with the pizza. Eventually, your body *will* win. It will patiently get louder and louder until you start to listen.

Perhaps you feel melancholy. What needs to change in your life? Where are you missing out on joy? What calling are you failing to follow? You can ignore it, and you can self-medicate to cover up the feeling. But if the message is ignored, your melancholy can transform into full-blown depression or addiction until it gets your attention. "Change your life!" it will scream—and you may no longer have a choice.

The thing about listening to the body is that the more you do it, the easier it gets. We are constantly given these very real cues. Most of the time the solution the body is asking for is quite clear and straightforward. Rest more. This is a good/bad idea. Change the way you're doing this.

Sometimes the cues have a more esoteric message, and it isn't always black and white. For example, have you ever had neck pain that you couldn't quite shake, and it suddenly went away when you made a change in your life? Or have your low back or hips started to hurt when you move to a new location or you're going through some major life change?

The body hosts every part of you—your fears, your resistances, your emotions and soul. When things are flowing easily, your body usually feels it. When you are afraid, your body feels it. When you are happy, your body feels it.

Because those less obvious cues are a little harder to see, it can sometimes be useful to spend time asking the part of your body that is giving you grief what it needs. I'm offering a suggestion to help you get in touch with those messages. Your subconscious speaks to you through your body. You are opening a doorway for the part of you that already knows the answer to speak more directly.

(TECHNIQUE) ## Talking to Your Body

For this technique, have a pen and paper next to you so when you finish the embodied meditation you can transition directly into writing.

Lie or sit in a comfortable position and relax. Start to slow your breath and come into the present moment. Scan your body to see if there's an area that pops into your awareness. It may or may not be the area that you expect, but be sure it's an area that would like some attention. Simply breathe and give awareness and presence to this area. Now, silently ask, "What do you need from me?" Then drop any expectations about getting an answer. Simply let that area be seen and heard. You may have some intuition or thought pop in your mind that clues you in, and you may not. Know that your loving presence is helping to heal that area whether your mind consciously knows the answers or not. Continue to breathe and feel the fluctuations that occur in that area as you give it your awareness. Notice the variance in the levels of discomfort or tightness. Let that area be exactly how it is in the moment. Watch and listen as if a good friend is venting her problems to you. Be fully present with this part of yourself.

When you feel like you've given ample time to the area, slowly open your eyes and write down, "What does (this area of my body) need? What would (you) like to say?" Allow yourself to write whatever comes through. Spend a good two to five minutes receiving whatever that part of your body is communicating. Try to stay in the meditative and receptive part of your mind as the words flow from your body, through your hand and onto the paper.

When you feel complete, read over what you've written.

Life is What You Make It

Have you ever read a "Choose Your Own Adventure" book? I used to love these stories when I was a child. Was I ever satisfied with choosing one adventure and stopping there? No way! If I chose a path that had a happy ending, I still went back to read about the disaster, and if I died, well, I went back and found my way to the happy ending. The diversity and unfolding of the scenes were exciting and interesting, and I enjoyed them all. Life doesn't happen all that differently. You can always go back and choose a new path, seek another adventure.

An old belief pattern I carried with me for a long time is, "If I don't make the right decisions, my life won't go as well." This pattern is the plight of someone who has control issues, someone who has carried the belief that mistakes are tragic paths into disaster. Because this has been an undercurrent of my perception of reality, I have created many situations that make me face those fears. Life has handed me numerous opportunities to make decisions and take action when I didn't have a clearly lit path in front of me.

As soon as I step in a direction—any direction—life begins to unfold in ways that support whatever decision I have made. If after awhile I don't like how I feel after walking a particular path, I can make a new decision and be just as supported on that path.

If I stay frozen and indecisive for too long, life starts to carry me in a direction of *its* choosing (often while I kick and scream, fearing what is next). Sometimes life's plan has a current so strong there's no choice but to surrender to it.

My hope is to help you feel the current and the direction that life is heading so you can learn to flow with it more easily. The expansive "yes" that you get when you are at a crossroads is a good indication of the easiest direction to follow. We are beings who crave experience, and often on some level we actually *want* a certain amount of struggle in order to learn and grow. Easy doesn't always equate with best. There have been times when I have gotten a "yes" and the path has been quite rocky. It's an adventure and a lesson rather than pure ease. But I find that at the end of that bumpy road, an even better and richer experience awaits me. Sometimes the most difficult hiking trails are the ones that lead you into the most beautiful parts of nature: the stunning waterfall or the vista overlooking the ocean. You get to see and experience things that strike awe within you. To me, the feeling of awe is about as close as we can get to the truth of who we really are.

Usually, when you follow your inner knowing, you are in the middle of the stream of life where things unfold rather easily and quickly. When we resist that knowing or we try to swim against the current, the force of life will increase to uproot us and carry us into the stream regardless of our decisions and preferences.

To follow the current of life is to drop your resistance to what is occurring. Because many of us are trained to do everything but listen to our inner guidance, it can take practice to re-engage that part of ourselves. But as soon as you become reacquainted with that inner compass, you need only to decide to follow it.

The Habit of Negative Thinking

Often we are addicted to suffering. We want to find our way toward a happier and better life, but we hold ourselves back from experiencing joy. We have access to joyful things in every moment. Even in the depths of our despair, the sun is rising and setting, the birds are chirping, someone loves us. We have food and shelter. We have the time and the desire to devote to inward seeking and to feeling good. Arguably, everyone reading this has more resources than most of the people on the planet.

Because of how we are built, we see what is not working in our environment. We see where action may be needed or a threat may actually exist. These observations are critical to our biological survival and are completely normal. What is not useful, however, is the amount of energy and time we spend talking and thinking about these things. I have caught myself, when engaging with certain friends, digging inside to find something that isn't going well so we can relate, discuss and problem-solve. I feel the urge to be in the mess sometimes. We really do bond over suffering, and if you are part of a social group that tends to problem-solve, you may find yourself talking about problems more than successes, joys and dreams.

Notice when you begin to complain or vent. Again, nothing is wrong with either of these activities and, in fact, sometimes we need a friend or a sounding board to help us navigate. But also be aware that if you have a habit of talking about your problem, seeing what is wrong and complaining, you are reinforcing and strengthening that pattern in your brain.

What if you practiced resisting the urge to talk about what's wrong, and instead found an inspiring or lovely connection with others? What if your negative thoughts could be interrupted and you remembered something that you were grateful for instead? Practice pausing a little more frequently and start bringing your subconscious habits into view. As soon as you become aware of them, they begin to shift.

Thinking versus Feeling

Check in with yourself the next time you have a problem or an undesired emotion. Notice if you can stay in the sensation of pure feeling instead of spending your time thinking about the scenario that revealed that feeling. Train your mind to feel rather than think. When you are in pure sensation, you can relax more, and the emotions can exist and express without judgment. This is how you integrate feelings. Once you stop judging or empowering the stories that bring the emotions to light, you can simply notice the energy that makes up the feeling. When anger, sadness and shame, for instance, have no charge around them, they lose their power over you. They can move and exist without struggle—along with your joy and freedom and confidence.

(TECHNIQUE) **Changing the Habit**

Start paying attention to your thoughts and your words. What are you saying to yourself all day long? To others? When you catch yourself saying or thinking something unkind to yourself or others, or when you express a complaint or grievance, try to interrupt yourself. Notice these tendencies with wonder and interest, and try to withhold judgment. Celebrate that you were able to notice this totally human and normal way of being. Be grateful that this pattern is no longer subconscious.

Now choose to replace that thought or those words with something more akin to how you actually want to feel.

If you tend to think, "I'm no good at this. Why do I even try?" Decide instead to think (and feel) "I'm amazing and I have so much to offer this world." Simply notice how this shift alters your experience. Notice the expansiveness of making that choice. It is completely normal to sometimes feel as though you're lying to yourself when you begin this. If you have years of practice thinking of yourself as a failure, it may take some time to convince your subconscious that you are amazing. But stay with the practice daily, and you will see your thought patterns improve. Practice this whenever you can. Make it into a fun game and see where it takes you.

Drop the Technique

I am a thinker. I like to explore and test things out and try on different techniques and practices to see how they affect my body and my nervous system. It's fun for me to see what helps connect me to my true nature and what things bring me out of it. Because I love exploring techniques, I can sometimes block my own progression toward relaxation because the technique takes a bit of effort and concentration, no matter how much the exercise is designed to serve the nervous system.

Sometimes the best technique is no technique. It's okay to just feel yourself relax and enjoy the present moment. If having no technique is too much for you at first, you can make the art of relaxing into a game, where you feel yourself relax and melt more and more.

Concentration can sometimes create tension. If you notice that your jaw and face are still holding on as you are consciously relaxing, you may benefit from dropping the need for whatever technique you are working on. The whole point is to assist in progressively relaxing tension to allow your vitality to come through. So check in once in a while to see how well your favorite techniques are actually working to promote a more relaxed, expanded and vibrant state.

Weathering the Storm: A Little Help from Your Friends

Though the road toward liberation is ultimately an inside job—one that requires silence, reflection, feeling and listening—sometimes the best thing you can do is to remember the connectedness you have with others.

You are not alone. And when life crushes you, at times no amount of meditation, breathing, yoga or nature can calm you. Sometimes life picks you up and thrashes you around, and your mind and body go into panic or grief. These are the moments when calling on others and being willing to receive from them is essential.

I had a poignant moment one night that reminded me of the importance of leaning on others. My mind was spinning with the chaos of transition, and I couldn't sleep or calm myself through any of my regular methods. I felt lost and afraid, and even a little ashamed that I couldn't work through these feelings and settle myself down. I am, after all, supposedly an expert at this nervous system stuff, right?

I finally got out of bed and went downstairs to pet my cat and cry. My partner heard me, came downstairs and started rubbing my back to soothe me. Immediately, I felt my entire being let go. My shoulders relaxed, my body surrendered and my mind was at last quieting. He brought me back upstairs and tucked me into bed. The cats hopped up on the bed, offering their help as well. I was able to feel the magic that happens when you are tangibly surrounded by love. I had no idea how much I needed the support at that moment. I have been self-reliant my entire life, and I forgot that sometimes all we need is to be willing to receive the support and encouragement of people (or beings) who love us. For once, I dropped my responsibility, my control, my need to live up to my own expectations. I simply allowed myself to be weak and supported by someone else. I just needed my family.

7

Enhancing Positive Feelings
Getting the Right Nutrition

We have all heard the phrase, "You are what you eat." Most of us haven't taken that phrase very seriously. And if we have, we have applied it to the food choices we make and left it at that.

Nutrition refers to *everything* we ingest. We get our energy from the food we eat, and we process and eliminate the things in the food that we don't need. But we get far more energy from our breath, and the exhalation expels more toxic waste than any other system in our bodies. Without the exhalation, we would quickly die from carbon dioxide poisoning.

On a more subtle level, our thoughts, our feelings, our environment are constantly feeding us. We hear and see these subtle cues all day long. Our cells respond to all types of nutrition. There have been various studies showing how plants change according to subtle aspects of their growing environment. Even if the soil and sunlight are equal, the plant that is cared for lovingly will be healthier and more robust than the one that is neglected or treated with malice. Through Dr. Masaru Emoto's work we've learned that the same thing happens with water at a molecular level, based on the emotional environment or types of music played around the water.

Our extracellular matrix (the environment of each of our cells) is a gelatinous form of water. Imagine what is happening to us at a cellular level if we are constantly berating ourselves or filled with doubt or guilt or shame. Imagine what happens if we feel vibrant, loving and confident? If you summon these feelings now, you can feel what physically and systemically happens to your body.

The way we relate to ourselves and the environment we create speaks to our habits. If you get into the habit of eating nutritious food most of the time, and you realize that you feel better, it becomes more compelling to make that your usual choice. And when you get into a habit of speaking kindly to yourself and choosing to find joy or peace where you can, you will notice vast improvements in how you feel. And practice makes it a habit.

Spend more time noticing what you are thinking. Observe your self-talk, or catch yourself when you start to speak or think negatively about your situation. Is there a gift in the situation that you're overlooking? Can you decide to change the channel of your mind to something you love or feel grateful for? I'm not suggesting you wear rose-colored glasses and ignore real problems, but notice if you are spending more time thinking about the problems than is productive. Many of us spend too much time spinning our wheels.

Notice how you feel after you spend an hour watching the news. Now ask yourself if that hour of time yielded an hour's worth of useful information. Likely, you got the gist of the news story in the first couple of minutes. You might choose to read the headlines on a news site just long enough to be informed without surrounding yourself with the fear and doom you are being fed. What if instead, you spent that extra 50 minutes listening to music that you love or watching a show that brings you joy? Consider how you feed yourself on a daily basis and make informed choices.

At some point, I made the decision that feeling good outweighed excessive knowledge, so I stopped listening to NPR every day. I stopped reading all of the news stories online. I have enough exposure to social media and to people who I trust to analyze the news of the day. If a story interests me, I explore it, but for the most part I no longer like the vibration that the news creates.

When I decided to stop listening to the news, one other thing became quite clear; the stories hardly ever changed. I was listening to people say the same things again and again, with maybe one or two additional pieces of useful information. The news wasn't giving me more knowledge; it was simply creating stronger pathways toward a vibration that I didn't like. It was making the fear and depression and anger signals stronger.

Removing the news from my information load was a simple choice I made to change my experience in the world. This doesn't mean that I shy away from "negative" things or that I'm too fragile to handle it, but being attuned to a way of being that doesn't have that noise in the background all the time has definitely created a more enjoyable experience. I prefer to feel good and to amplify that feeling by making choices that support that feeling. There is no right or wrong in how you decide to experience life, but there are easier and more difficult paths. Most of us would like to feel better than we do. Look at the choices you make, and feel empowered that you have a say in how your life plays out.

Choosing Joy

I am very much of the mindset that every single feeling has validity. Every emotion has its beautiful place in our experience, and they are all worthy of being felt and heard. They all have messages to send to us, and they all have value.

We accumulate so many layers of unfelt and unexpressed feelings that it is essential to our well-being that we get to know and feel them. Walking into the dark forest is a necessary part of our journey as humans. Everyone's journey is essentially their own, and it is up to each person to walk through it, crawl through it, fly above it or find a different route.

Some people charge ahead with abandon, not caring how lost they get, but knowing (hoping) they will get to the other side. Others step cautiously, explore a little and then walk back out for a while. Some people spend most of their lives outside the forest and only go in kicking and screaming because life has pushed them there and they can no longer avoid it. There is no wrong way to navigate and experience the fullness and richness of you and your unique life experience.

When you have a sharp and active mind, it can sometimes get creative, convincing you that you need to feel some of your feelings more than you actually do. If you have a large amount of a certain emotion that you haven't yet felt and expressed, your mind will create stories and scenarios that will bias you toward noticing them.

In cases of maladapted alarm systems, we begin to see things through a foggy lens. Our past experiences and traumas will intervene with our present experience and will create the "what ifs," the worry and the fear. Anger, frustration, hurt, or the pain of rejection may also be speaking to us even when the situation at hand isn't actually the cause of those feelings.

Again, I urge you to feel those feelings. These moments are golden opportunities to dissipate some of the held-in emotions. But at the same time, become aware that the feeling you are having is a result of a creative thought pattern. Recognize that it's an exaggeration, and though the feelings are strong and real, the situation might not actually warrant that response.

Once you allow the "loudest" emotion to flow through you, return to your breath and notice that you have access to *all* of your feelings and vibrations at any time. If you can easily summon joy and peace, go ahead and do it. Choose joy.

I know that when you're in the midst of something that is compelling and strong, it may seem that your current situation justifies your feelings. I am not trying to convince you that it's wrong to feel afraid, sad, angry, depressed, agitated—it's right to feel all those ways. But remember: feelings are energy, and they are fleeting and mobile. When a feeling gets "stuck" it's usually because our thoughts continue to energize it. We continue to create scenarios in our mind that are beyond what is actually happening, to keep us in the feeling. Again, there is no judgment on this process. In fact, it's necessary sometimes to go down the rabbit hole. But know that as you're following your thoughts in this way, you are making a choice to do so on some level. The inertia may be so strong that it doesn't feel like a choice, but it is. At some point, hopefully when the inertia has weakened, it becomes easier to make a new choice. I choose to live in a more joyful state.

Yes, I have a problem to solve, and I feel overwhelmed. Yes, I'm afraid or angry or sad. Yes, I feel like my life might be spiraling out of control. I still choose to find the joy and peace that I know reside within me.

If you watch a toddler express his feelings, he throws himself onto the ground and wails as if his life will end because of what happened. He kicks, he screams, he feels despair with every cell of his body. And when he's done, he gets a drink from his juice box and plays with his blocks. It's over. He returns to joy.

This process is our nature. We have the same ability as adults, no matter what our perception of a situation is. (Perhaps, if we kicked and screamed more, we would process faster?) Your mind will tell you, "Yes, but you have problems to solve that aren't yet handled. You are responsible for providing and caring for your family. These are *real* problems in the *real* world."

Your mind is not making this up. Your mind is logical and wants to solve a problem. It wants to protect you from harm and make sure you survive.

Let your mind solve problems by doing what it does best: analyzing, assessing, and taking logical steps. The mind is *not* best used for creating the "what-if" scenarios and possible outcomes that don't actually exist, or clinging to past hurts that are impeding your progress. This part of the mind is simply creating roadblocks to your joyful, in-the-moment experience. So unless you're writing a disaster movie or apocalyptic novel, let that part of your mind sit on the sidelines for a while.

I am not here to admonish the mind. It exists as a miraculous part of our experience and its abilities are amazing and unfathomable. I *love* my mind. The mind is simply an overgrown and untended garden. It needs care and pruning and watering. Pull out the weeds so there's more room for the flowers. Let the garden know that you're there to care for it and with some love, it can be one of the most beautiful parts of your home on this planet.

If you love thinking and knowing and solving as much as I do, use your mind to play a game with yourself that lets it sort the actual assessment and actions from the past and future fiction it has created. Let your mind notice the full and true experience of now, or challenge it to search its archives for memories of past happiness or loving moments. Let your mind work in favor of your best experience.

Give your mind tools for and reminders of how it can work optimally for you. Because the mind likes to create, let it create for you in a positive way. When you've given yourself a finite number of options, ask your mind to come up with some other wildly creative possibilities.

If your mind has used the past to predict the future, ask it to come up with some other scenarios. Dare to feel the outcome of those scenarios with equal vigor. If your mind has told you, "What if I fail?" start to ask, "What if I succeed?" Play a game of opposites with your mind. Choose to feel and experience the joy that these other scenarios could bring.

You may convince yourself that you're just playing with fantasy and that this exercise isn't based in reality. Well, guess what? Your negative scenarios aren't based in reality, either. You've just become really good at convincing yourself that they are.

Leaning into Positivity

It's our birthright to be happy and enjoy life, and it's been established that we have a natural bias toward negative thoughts for the purposes of survival. This natural inclination needs to be countered if we want to see real changes in our habits and in our brains. We have a reached a point when positive neuroplasticity is well documented—it's useful and it works. For people who haven't spent time listening inwardly, moving directly toward "happiness" can sometimes cause denial or repression of the feelings that are naturally occurring. They might also feel worse about themselves if they are unable to summon the feelings of happiness in those moments.

Both science and esoteric teachings give us examples and methods that encourage us to gravitate to positive thinking. Negative thinking truly has an oppressive effect on the psyche and well-being. But emotions are there to be felt and acknowledged. All feelings expand us and make us richer.

If you have a hard time navigating the difference between feeling and thinking, perhaps when you are depressed or angry, slow down your thoughts through breathing and returning to the present moment. Thoughts fuel feelings, so choose to slow the train down. Once you slow your mind down a little, simply shift toward feeling the sensation in your body and allow that emotional expression to move through your system.

Expression can come in the form of sound, tears, or movement. If you're angry, allow yourself to scream into a pillow or writhe around or stomp your feet or pound your bed, but keep the awareness on the energy and the feeling. If thoughts try to put gasoline on the fire, acknowledge them, breathe and let them pass through. Shift back to feeling the sensation in your body and letting it express.

Once you acknowledge and express the feeling, you create more space. This is when I suggest you take the golden opportunity to summon something positive to fill that space. One of John Barnes' reminders is that "nature abhors a void." If there is space something will fill it, so choose to fill your newly opened territory with something that you desire more of in your life.

I am a huge fan of all the books, researchers and mystically-inclined people who tout the benefit of positive affirmation, changing our vibration and leaning toward love and happiness. As long as we have cleared out subconscious beliefs that sabotage our desires, these things work. The key to the effectiveness of these techniques, at least in my own experience, is to acknowledge, feel and express the subconscious "saboteurs" and then summon the *feeling* of the positive vibration or quality that we wish to embody.

Words alone will not do the job. If you say over and over, "I love and accept myself," there is very little power or juice behind it—especially if those moments of "I hate myself" are potent with feeling. You need to *truly feel* as if you love and accept yourself as you say those words. You need the power of feeling behind it. And the stronger your saboteur is, the more powerful and practiced your feelings of love and acceptance must be. If you have a hard time feeling love for yourself, then summon a sense of love for something or someone else. The feeling is the same either way.

Let's try this technique to work with something almost everyone I know struggles with: financial abundance. If you have a daily practice of repeating the mantra "I am abundant," but fear tends to come up whenever you look at your bills or your bank account, or you feel your body tighten when you have to pay for things, those energies have a lot of feeling behind them.

One suggestion is to add emotion and a visual to your daily practice. As you say, "I am abundant," see yourself showered with whatever abundance looks and feels like for you. Make the dream quite big. Feel the decadence and ease that this abundance brings you. How would you feel if you had everything you needed and wanted all of the time?

Bring forth that feeling and practice keeping it as big, as clear and as strong as you can.

Another thing you can try is bringing change to the moments you are paying bills or buying things. Notice the tendency you might have to tense up, and choose in that moment to bring forth the feeling and the belief you're working on in your daily practice. Feel grateful that you are able to pay for whatever it is you are purchasing, even if it's a minimum balance payment or buying a simple item like toilet paper. Start to replace the fear with the knowledge that you are already abundant and that all your needs are met.

Finally, try inserting moments into your day where you pause and feel the awe of the richness all around you. Nature is an easy exhibition of abundance. Look at the miraculous technologies you have: a television, a cell phone, a car, a home. See the robust blooming of the flowers. Gratefully eat the decadent and amazing food that's in front of you. Feel the richness of laughter with a good friend, or the ability to rest on the weekend.

The more you practice, the better you'll get at changing your scenario. The more you focus on your abundance, the more it appears. Your mind will want to play an important role in figuring out how this is possible, or it will tell you all the reasons it isn't possible. But feelings are bigger than thoughts. Use them wisely.

One final note: There is a natural tendency to get distracted. Changing your brain and your vibration takes commitment and discipline. Create a daily practice and dedicate yourself to it for longer than you might believe you need. Again, think of those neural pathways as rivers. The deepest rivers were the ones that your old tendencies carved out, so you need to commit to digging the new ditches deep enough that the water flows through the new avenues more easily than it does the old pathways.

"Practice and all is coming." — Pattabhi Jois

Finding Your Way to Alignment

The most exciting part of this life journey is the knowledge that we get to choose to be here however we want to be here. There is no one path. It's impossible to "mess it up." We get to have experiences and learn what we like and what we don't like. We get to become more attuned to what expands us and what contracts us, what feels good and in alignment and what doesn't. Feeling unaligned allows us to have a reference point for how we feel when we are aligned. Those experiences are valuable and completely necessary.

For reasons way too complex to start unraveling here, we have trained our minds into believing in right and wrong. We have learned to feel guilt and shame when we do things that we perceive as wrong. Reality has no concept of right and wrong. Instead, it is either aligned with love and the truth of who we are or it is not. One of my favorite reminders of this is something Dr. Ravi Ravindra shared during a lecture I attended: "At its etymological root, the word 'sin' means 'to miss the mark.' "

Do we shame the toddler who falls down while learning to walk? Do we pile guilt onto the baby who isn't able to roll over yet? We are learning the skill of alignment and flow. Start dropping the shame and guilt and try dusting yourself off. Learn from your fall, get back up and try again. Life becomes a lot more fun, and the lessons can be learned more quickly.

What would it be like if we could all look at the politicians and see them as people who are trying to learn alignment? What if we could remember that they have to fall a few more times before they learn this skill? What if we were able to keep in mind that humanity is flowing toward growth, and that the inevitable progression is that we *will* learn to align with love? Just as the baby *will* learn to roll over, crawl, walk and speak, we will eventually grow into beings that learn that it's easier to get around when we are aligned. We won't crawl and fall forever.

We are moving toward alignment with love, compassion, ease and grace. These qualities feel better and they make life easier. Once we understand how bad it feels when we are contracted and small, we will start making the choice to feel expanded and good. It's our nature—it's who we are. Once we remove the belief systems about what right and wrong actually are and once we drop the judgment, guilt and shame about making restricting choices, we can speed up this process both within ourselves and for humanity at large.

Tuning into Reality

Most of the time, we forget who and what we are. Our minds have assessed, broken down and evaluated the world through our individual lens. And for the most part, we have believed that our perception is the truth.

When we learn to relax the nervous system and let life stream through us, we get small glimpses into something that is a bit closer to the actual truth. Reality is expansive and energized and alive and lovely. A good reminder for us is that when we feel anything other than expansive, it's likely that we are tuning into our thought streams and beliefs. We get so accustomed to the way those patterns cause us to feel that we may believe it's our reality.

This is not to say that when these restrictive feelings arise we should just pretend they aren't there. Whenever we increase our resonance with love and our true essential nature, we create more room for the unloved and fearful aspects of ourselves to be revealed. Those feelings and old thought patterns, and even our deepest, darkest shadow aspects, need to be seen and loved. Often the parts of ourselves that are harder to face don't start showing up until after we've worked hard to soothe our systems.

When you are experiencing a vibration that is contracted or dull, go ahead and feel it, but also remember that the sensation in front of you, no matter how pervasive or big, is not the whole picture. You are expanded and vibrant and dynamic and joyous—that part of you is standing in the wings, waiting to embrace the other part. Even if the vibration isn't accessed easily in that moment, it helps to remember that it's still a large and vital part of who you are.

Think of yourself as a radio tuning dial. There's a lot of fuzz where several things are happening simultaneously. Once you hear a frequency coming into tune, you play with the dial until you hear the song or dialogue more clearly. Your emotional landscape operates in the same manner. Many things are occurring in each moment. Sometimes an event or a thought causes a particular "station" to get louder and clearer, so you tune into it and then you can clearly hear and experience that specific feeling.

Some of us live in places where the only stations that come in loud and clear are the ones we don't like. Yet rather than work with the static that's affecting the station we do like, we settle for crappy music. It takes effort and finesse to get the fuzzy station that's playing music we love to become clearer. But once it's set just right, we can program it as a pre-set station and tune in at any time. It benefits you to become skilled at turning the dial and changing the channel to something you prefer. It truly is that simple. Get used to hearing some fuzz and exerting more effort for a while until you can simply change to your favorite station when you decide to.

When fear or anger or jealousy or sadness show up, tune in so that you can hear what is being presented to you. See if the news story is worth listening to before you move onto the next thing. Decide if you like that song or that particular type of music today. When you tune in entirely to the feeling, you might quickly get strong enough information to decide whether or not to change the station. If you keep it on that low, fuzzy, not-quite-tuned-in level or you turn the volume way down, you can't hear the song well enough to make that decision, so it just keeps humming along in the background. Tune it in, turn it up, and then move on.

Once you get better at recognizing the feeling, you generally won't feel inclined to hang with it quite as long as you needed to before you became familiar with it. If you have heard a particular pop song so many times that you only need to hear one or two notes before recognizing it, you can quickly make an assessment about whether you do or don't want to listen to it. If it's a song you've only heard once or twice, or if you're not sure how you feel about it, you might listen a bit longer and, sometimes, keep the song on until the end. There is no right or wrong—there are only experiences and choices. You decide if you've heard the call of anger, depression or fear clearly and often enough to change the station.

It takes motivation to want a different experience, and it takes practice. Life is wide open for you. Do you want to feel more of who you are? Practice feeling it. Don't shy away from the shadowy aspects of yourself or others—see them, listen to them, and love them the best way you know how. But I highly suggest learning to change the channel and tuning into stations that you prefer. Love, peace, joy, kindness, beauty, gratitude, abundance, health—those are closer to the truth.

Strengthening the Signal

Many of the techniques I offer in this book work at the level of the nervous system, and practicing any of them or any technique that makes you feel better and more expanded, is a good way to become more attuned to love.

Meditation, relaxation, joyous activities, music, great food, sex, gratitude lists, loving exchanges with friends and family—the list of ways to strengthen the pathway toward expansion and joy is vast. Make a conscious effort to incorporate some of the things you enjoy into your life every single day. And when you are doing these things, make another conscious decision to enjoy them and soak in their vibration fully and completely. Call on your inner child and experience those moments in full vigor and awe, just as your younger self would.

If you're feeling a little more stuck and can't quite summon the joy in the regular everyday ways, I suggest utilizing one of the many resources that are geared toward raising your vibration: inspirational talks, group online seminars and meditations, going to church or a meditation group, whatever lifts you up. Do not underestimate the power that comes with combining forces with others. Anyone who meditates can attest to how much deeper the meditation becomes when they are in a group. Singers can tell you that playing and singing with others amplifies their experience. Praying with others can raise your vibration tenfold over praying alone. Laughing with a group at a theater makes the joy greater than laughing alone. Yoga classes allow for higher levels of strength than a home practice.

Even as an introverted empath, I have countless experiences where group energy fields have created positive changes in how I feel. (Of course, I have also experienced the opposite if the group field isn't in alignment with what I am looking for in that moment.)

Because I mostly like to be alone when I am not working, I do fewer group activities than many of my friends and colleagues. If you are tired or prefer to be alone, use online resources, books or music to help lift you up. For lifting my spirits, my favorite resource is the internet where many generous teachers offer blogs, videos and audio files. Their words lift me up, but greater than that, they exude their high vibration and share their expanded state of being with me every time I listen or read or watch. I can even keep them on in the background as I get ready for my day or wind down or do chores, and I feel better. Listening to music that you love can accomplish the same.

Think about how you feel when news or commercials are on in the background. It's very different than when your favorite music is playing. Start to notice how you actually feel rather than doing what you think you should be doing.

I have always valued my mind. Now that I know the mind's purpose, I actually value it more. The mind is a beautiful tool for critical thought and problem solving, and for expressing and creating through language. When I use my mind this way instead of relying on it to control my life, wonderful things start to happen. It thrives when put to good use.

Before this shift in perception, my mind was giving me false problems and worries and unlikely scenarios to deal with. My thoughts would create emotions that weren't appropriate for the real situation in front of me. Now, I get to enjoy my mind and put it to good, creative use. I get to see it freak out once in awhile and go into its old role as the manager of my life, but instead of blindly following along, I can smile, take a breath and just corral it back into its rightful and useful place.

Where can you make an easy choice to feel better? How can you strengthen the sensations that you want to feel and tune away from feelings that you have grown too accustomed to? Remember, having those lower vibrational feelings is necessary, and they will present themselves throughout your life. Just be aware that they aren't the whole story, and they aren't indicative of who you really are. Start to notice that you have access to the reality of love, joy and expansion and, with practice and compassion, you will get better at living there more often. You will be able to tune into those feelings whenever you decide to.

8

Taking Action

Bringing Your Skills into the World

A few years ago, I worked with a wonderful coach who has vast expertise in helping people in positions of leadership. As part of our time together, she conducted a few personality-style tests. I was not too surprised to find out that I tend toward a more visionary and idealistic style. As she pointed out, "You and your friends can sit around and create solutions to all the world's problems. But nothing ever happens because you lack the tendency to put those ideas into action."

She didn't say this to criticize me. She simply was pointing out that collaboration is a useful tool and that I should maximize my unique skills but let someone who's good at implementing plans take on the action steps.

This was great advice, and I resonated with the awareness that I am a wonderful thinker, planner, and researcher. I come up with new ideas and options all the time. I get very excited about something, and I can create opportunities pretty easily. What is difficult for me is actually following through on one of those options and moving forward with real action steps toward what I want.

If you're an action-oriented person, this may sound strange and foreign to you. My mom is a perfect example of someone who is amazingly skilled at crossing things off lists and getting things done. She's organized and efficient and doesn't think twice before calling the cable repairman to come fix the TV. I can spend hours online researching the best repair service, wondering when would be a convenient time for an appointment, then writing it down as a "to do" item. I find other more interesting things to occupy my time, and put off the easy task of picking up the phone and calling to schedule the repair.

I envy this skill of taking action because it's a muscle that I have not developed as well. I have realized that even though it's not my usual tendency to take immediate action, it's a skill I want to improve. So the solution is simple: Practice taking immediate action when something is in your awareness. For me, this means fighting inertia and habit and (depending on the situation) pushing through fear.

When it comes to "following the feeling," opportunities present themselves regularly in my life. I often procrastinate action. I weigh the options, I research and wait for the signal to get clearer. I've seen these opportunities fade and the glimmer wear off if I wait long enough. Then another shiny new opportunity comes along.

As I've said before, there is no right or wrong way to do things, and every time you miss a wave of opportunity, another will soon follow. But life is a lot more dynamic and fun if you start riding the waves instead of just watching them go by. Because I've had many experiences of waiting before acting, I've seen how the door is open for a limited amount of time before it closes, and the next door looks brighter. If I want to have a particular experience, it becomes crucial to take action *while* the option is bright.

I am constantly ready to relocate—move to a new town, new city, start a new life. The operative words are *ready to*. Any time I travel and have a positive experience, that place gets added to my list of next places to live. I research jobs, the city, housing, everything about the place. In some cases, I've gone so far as to get my professional license in that state. I take preliminary action steps. But actually moving to the new area doesn't usually happen. At this point, any time I tell someone

I'm moving, they just smile and let me talk about the exciting new life-adventure that's in my mind. I guess I must *love* to plan, and create, because I have all sorts of great lives that got started in so many different places doing so many different things. Those multiverse Lisa Wests are having a blast, I'm sure.

Though this process may have caused me to miss out on parts of life that I haven't yet encountered, I have gained an incredible amount of trust in the way the universe works. I have personally seen how new opportunities are always presenting themselves. If you don't walk through one door, maybe the next one will be even better.

There has been value in my process, and I don't regret a moment. I can see, however, that if you want to keep the flow of dynamic life moving, taking action is necessary. We have to do our part.

I don't use a "technique" when it comes to taking action because the only way to truly get better at it is to *act*. Feel the resistance, hear the words of procrastination, recognize second guessing—but do it anyway.

Taking action on smaller things can help break the habit of inaction. Make that repair call as soon as something breaks, or click the "purchase" button on the web page you've had open for two weeks with the book you want to order on it. Make the doctor appointment you should have scheduled three months ago. Practice until it becomes easier and notice that the world does work better when you take action.

Trust

When I started musing about this book, I felt the concept was so simple. Get quiet, feel your feelings, then follow what they guide you to do. There isn't a whole lot to more to say. It's self-evident and straightforward.

What isn't quite as simple is recognizing and trusting the information you are getting. If you were raised to trust yourself and your feelings, you are a step ahead in this process. Most of us have been taught to ignore our instincts and inner guidance in service of following rules or doing what is "logical."

When I first began noticing my intuition, it was difficult for me to distinguish between my inner knowing and what my mind was telling me. Sometimes the voices sounded the same to me, or my mind was so conditioned that I would confuse familiarity with knowing.

My best advice is to start by noticing how each message *feels*. If you are deciding between two menu items, for example (a great and easy place to start), see which one seems more relaxed or more exciting. If you're surprised by the answer, chances are it is something to trust. Once you memorize how it feels to make the right decision, it gets easier.

Another way to practice trusting is to feel what it's like when you do something aligned with your values and how it feels when you don't. That is a louder expression of a similar feeling, so it is a good way to recognize your inner cues.

For example, if you have a glass bottle and there's a trash can nearby, and you value recycling, try to throw the bottle away and see how you feel. Then take it out of the garbage and walk across the room to the recycling bin and see how that feels. If people are gossiping about someone, see what it's like to go along with it and how it feels to disengage from it. If you are passionate about racial equality and someone makes a derogatory racial comment, how does it feel to stay silent versus speaking up? The internal signals our core values give us are usually pretty strong and easily noticeable. We don't always follow those cues, often because we want to feel culturally accepted, but we certainly feel them.

Inner knowing and intuition have a similar, if subtler, feeling to them. When you know the right thing to do, your body relaxes, opens and feels more energized. When something isn't quite right, you know that too. I once saw a sign that read, "Say yes if it is a full-body yes. Everything else is a no."

I follow that advice regularly. My body knows. Your body knows. We just have to decide to trust what we are hearing and feeling. And then we need to follow through and take action in that direction.

Start Where it's Easy

Erich Schiffman suggests practicing your newly developed skills in situations that have relatively low stakes, such as, "Should I have the burger or the salad for lunch?" or "Which route should I take to work today?"

A great opportunity to practice this skill is when deciding whether or not to go to social events. When I feel an expansive feeling inside my body or excitement about something, then I can trust that spending time with people is a great thing for me to do. When I feel contracted or hesitant about going, it's usually a good idea for me to decline. This is easier said than done. It requires a willingness to know that you will not know how you feel until the moment comes around, which can make planning things a little tricky. My friends and I have an understanding with each other to allow some fluidity in our decision making the day of the event. Not all situations are as easy to change, especially if it's something that requires some advance planning. But even when you aren't feeling it for those types of events, and you go anyway, you do have the ability to make a shorter appearance or at least tell your loved ones that you're feeling a little tired. Often in those situations, I find that the group energy does lift me up and carry me through and I just take more downtime the next day.

(TECHNIQUE) **Feeling the Choices**

The first step to using this method is to utilize your skills to help thaw out fear. "Feeling Your Tension Level," "Letting Gravity Win" and "Feeling Present-moment Joy" are three techniques I have suggested, but if you have found a gem that works for you, I highly recommend using it. The point is to process and feel the fear until you can bring yourself into a state of relaxed and calm joy.

Once you are in a centered place, write down your dilemma and map out your potential action steps. This is a left-brained activity and is a perfect example of how your brain/mind can be used to do what it is built for: analyzing, assessing and sorting. Once you have a clear map of your options, bring yourself into a comfortable and relaxed position.

Begin to deepen your breath and bring yourself again into the calm, relaxed joy. Feel into that vibration. Continue to breathe slowly and notice the comfortable peace filling all of your cells and the space around you.

Next, gently call in the scenario that you are facing and see the options you have in front of you. Allow any fearful sensations or emotions to come up and just pass through this relaxed joy. Take your first option and picture yourself as if you have made that choice. How does it feel? Does it expand your relaxed and calm space? Does it tighten it up? Then let that scenario go.

Call in the next scenario, and again, feel what it is like to be in that option. Do you feel more expanded or more contracted? Does it increase your joy or have a shimmer of interest?

Continue this process through each option until you have a sense of which one seems to call you a little more, or feels bigger, more appealing or brighter. Trust your initial reaction. Notice when your mind wants to jump in. When it does, simply acknowledge it and let it pass through.

Additional notes:

I usually only spend a couple of moments with each of my options, as visceral and body-knowing reactions tend to happen pretty immediately. If I linger too long in the space of an option, sometimes I can let thoughts seep in and second-guess my gut reactions.

When the arguments for and against different options pop up, I quickly call up the one that shimmered the most and reconnect with the feeling of, "*Yes*, this feels right." Those arguments are the fear and resistance we have. They feel different than the knowing, but that difference is subtle and requires some practice and finesse to master. Fear feels tight. Knowing feels more open and relaxed. You can know something is right *and* feel fear about it at the same time. Most of us have had this experience: You know you have to act in a certain way, but you are afraid to do it. Your body and your being know it, even when your mind is skeptical.

Stretching Your Comfort Zone

As you learn to navigate life using your inner compass, you will sometimes be surprised by the information you receive. Our natural tendency from a biological standpoint is to stay within the confines of what is comfortable, to have a routine and to keep ourselves in situations that are predictable and easy to monitor. We lean toward safety. But this other part of us exists, the inner calling of our soul that wishes to expand and learn and grow. Fortunately for us, life is designed to automatically place us in situations that lie outside our comfort zones. Not one of us gets out of that experience, no matter how much we cling to our routines.

Even though our biology creates a sense of fear within us when we try something new, there is a flip side: excitement and anticipation. We are in the driver's seat and can decide which of these emotions receives our focus. Sometimes the experience of fear is exactly what we need, so we allow ourselves to feel it. Other times, we need the excitement of being alive, so that is what we feel instead.

Some of us are natural explorers and adventurers, and we have a powerful compulsion to shake things up at every opportunity, to see new things, to live life to its fullest. These people value freedom and novelty and excitement more than comfort and safety. Others prefer the experiences of peace, calm and quiet. No matter what our relationship is with change and expansion, we inevitably arc toward something new.

Have you ever had an experience where you are digging in your heels, resisting some type of change, fearing the worst, feeling helpless and hopeless and turned upside down, but when you reach the other side the experience ends up being better than you could have imagined?

Expansion *always* feels good after it happens. We are infinite beings, and our souls want to grow. What doesn't feel good is the resistance and the muck that gets stirred up within our psyches in order to move into an expanded state. When we get stuck, and when change drags us down, it is likely because we haven't accepted the change, haven't let go of the things we need to release in order for the change to occur and have not yet been able to bring ourselves into the new present moment.

Even tragic changes, like the death of a loved one or a battle with a severe illness, bring about expansion. These experiences bring us into the depths of our dark, unexpressed areas within and give us the opportunity to feel loss at a grand level. We grieve, and in that grief our hearts break. When our hearts break, the walls of protection and armor are completely shattered. New levels of vulnerability are accessed; huge doorways to compassion for others and ourselves are opened up. Our hearts expand. And in those quiet moments of clarity that appear within our personal storms, we feel our true nature at a depth we could not have experienced in any other way. We learn to let go and to surrender to the current of life because we have no other choice. We are reminded of our values and dreams. We gain a level of wisdom that we can carry forward into our lives and share with others: a wisdom that allows others to recognize and receive our compassion. Even when a hole remains in our hearts, we move forward transformed.

Stretching your comfort zone doesn't always have to occur in tragic or negative ways. You can and often naturally *do* stretch outside your comfort zone all the time. Trying out a new restaurant or traveling to a new place are some really great ways to expand. Changing the route you take to work grows you. So does trying a different walking path or moving to a new house. Having a baby or getting a new pet, going to lunch with a new friend—these experiences all lead you to parts of yourself that you wouldn't have encountered had you not breached your comfort zone.

When we are drawn toward anything spiritual or self-reflective, there tends to be a leaning in toward our shadow and the things that we still subconsciously deem "wrong" with ourselves. We forget that spiritual and personal growth also occur through joy and laughter and love and kindness and compassion. We often forget to feel good. Remember the neurological tendency toward avoiding pain and how that makes us focus more on the negative aspects of life? Just keep that in your pocket and occasionally ask yourself how you can seek joy or peace a little bit more right now.

Give yourself permission to feel good and to have the experience of expansion through the sunset you see in front of you, or the laughter with a good friend, or the delicious meal you are eating. Practice feeling good, and you will become better at it.

And don't forget to stretch out of your comfort zone in that direction, too. What can you do right now to feel *even better*?

Learning to Stretch

If stretching your comfort zone doesn't come easily to you, working with your body to help develop this skill can help on all other levels as well. Once you have become skilled at feeling relaxed under gentle circumstances, learn to stretch the relaxation "muscle" more so that you can better adapt to staying centered and calm even when life gets stressful. Begin teaching the nervous system to adapt to higher levels of stimulation. This can be done with any active physical exercise as long as you bring some mindfulness to the activity.

Yoga

Yoga is one of my favorite suggestions to use at this phase. Yoga is specifically geared to help tone the nervous system. Some types of yoga have more noticeable effects on the nervous system than others, but essentially all yoga is on some level positively impacting the nervous system—whether or not the teacher knows it.

The basic tenet of yoga *asana* (the physical postures) is to find a centered "seat" which is defined as equal parts steadiness and ease. Different teachers give different translations and interpretations as to what that means, but when you relate it to the autonomic nervous system, the "goal" is to find focused attention and ease within the posture. As you stretch your body and exert muscular contractions, you are creating inherent stress within your system. By coming into the present moment, breathing and finding a more relaxed state while you are in the posture, you are training your nervous system to be calmer in the face of stress.

Of course, yoga only works in this way if you are practicing being at ease while you are in the postures. Many of us exert a lot of effort to attain the pose but forget to find the ease. Over time, some of those postures do become easier, so an adaptation does occur, but you'll find that you can quicken the desired nervous system changes if you stay at a level where you can remain focused, find a smooth breath and ease in the face and eyes. When it becomes easy for you to do this, then it's a good idea to deepen the posture.

You aren't doing yoga to put your leg behind your head. Ideally, the person who puts their leg behind their head does so because this is the position that puts the appropriate amount of stress on their body. More often, it's a result of people overriding the actual "yoga" of the moment by trying to attain a posture. Most of you have no need to ever put your leg behind your head, unless you've been practicing yoga for so long or you're naturally so flexible, that any other hip opener isn't doing the job.

The other note about stress and yoga is that if you do tend to be a rather flexible person and don't feel much stress when you stretch, you likely will find more benefit (and a safer and better strategy for your body) in cultivating the stress out of strengthening postures. I say this as someone who could hang out in pigeon all day long, but if I have to stay in *utkatasana* (chair pose) for more than five breaths, my alarm systems want to go off. What that tells me is that if I want to actually get better at relaxing under stress, the strengthening postures are going to cultivate that for me more efficiently than the flexibility poses.

One more note about stability: If you want to be able to open and expand and stretch more, it is necessary to create a feeling of safety and stability. When your nervous system feels safe it allows more relaxation, which creates greater flexibility. Stability places the body in a safer mode to move into deeper postures without the risk of injury. This is why even the most flexible yogis can feel tight and stiff, even when they have a large range of motion. They are likely lacking the stability necessary for their body to truly relax and let go.

Another often neglected part of yoga that is extremely beneficial to the nervous system is *pranayama* (breathing techniques). Deep diaphragmatic breathing is one of the access points we have for stimulating the vagus nerve. This nerve is responsible for turning our systems from fight-or-flight into relaxation mode. Because yoga coordinates movement with deep breathing, it automatically starts to stimulate this nerve.

The *ujayi* breath, which is used in systems like *ashtanga* yoga, is a breath that has an airy sound to it. Constricting the back of the throat also stimulates the vagus nerve, so you get an even faster track toward relaxing your system. Most *vinyasa* or flow yoga classes are based off *ashtanga,* and many use this same type of breath. These practices are inherently challenging, so keep in mind that you may not be as skilled at relaxing your nervous system when you start navigating these postures. If you stay within your body's parameters, these practices are great at bringing you to your center.

Of course, yoga isn't the only way to do this—it's just built for it. Any challenge to your system, while breathing and staying centered and easy in your body, will create the same benefits. You can use physical exercise or practice staying calm in a stimulating environment such as an airport or traffic jam. It can be practicing ease while you are tackling a problem at work. The key is to be in the moment, breathe and relax a little more than you think you can.

Pushing Through Resistance

Sensations of fear or ennui you might be connecting with are often just simple resistance. Sometimes the resistance is well-intentioned and well-informed. The brakes you feel kicking on inside can be there to stop you from doing something that won't benefit you. More likely, the resistance feels like the inner two-year-old digging in her heels and saying, "I don't want to." Just as it's appropriate to guide the dirty toddler toward the bathtub or the tired child to bed, our inner adult sometimes needs to intervene when we're resisting.

I have resistance pretty much every time I have to make a phone call. I'm much more comfortable emailing, texting, doing things online so that I don't actually have to interact. As you can imagine, my business absolutely *relies* on returning clients' calls and discussing why they are coming to see me and to schedule appointments. Sometimes I can get it all done with texts and emails, but it's unrealistic (and often more time consuming) to set up an electronic exchange instead of picking up the phone and calling. It's the same with any other phone call—fixing a bill, renting an apartment, scheduling a hair appointment—it doesn't matter what it is, it's the action step that creates resistance. This is a clear example of me having resistance to something when there is obviously no danger. The phone calls help me move forward in my career and assist others with their healing.

We all find places that we resist what we know we need to do. Maybe we resist getting out of bed to meditate or exercise instead of hitting snooze, even though we are aware we had enough sleep. Maybe we resist going to the gym, even though we feel so much better after we do.

This type of resistance, the kind that really does feel the same to me as a little kid yelling "No!" probably developed because that child didn't feel she could win the fight very often. Sometimes, I let her win when the stakes are lower. It's okay that I got up thirty minutes later today and wrote a little less than I usually want to. I think it's important to let that part of myself feel acknowledged.

Other times, and most often, it's better to practice pushing through the resistance. The best way I've found to do this is to take a moment to breathe and feel that the resistance is there, and to feel the edges of the resistance soften with my kind awareness. Remember, you are dealing with your inner two-year-old, so be kind and let him/her express for a moment.

Procrastination is a very normal thing to do, and the feelings of inertia that lead to it are so very compelling. Feel those feelings. If you like engaging your mind, ask it where they come from. Sometimes that can help get the mind on board. But even if you have no idea why you feel this way, you can still acknowledge that the emotion is there, and you can *feel* it.

Anticipation of the next thing is almost always much worse than actually doing the next thing. So breathe and relax and feel into the present moment of what sensations procrastination brings up. For me, it feels like a micro-experience of fear/anxiety along with plain old laziness or stagnation. Try not to judge those feelings, just let them be.

After you breathe with it for a few moments, you will likely feel the resistance softening—you also may not. Summon up extra energy and make the choice to start doing the thing you are putting off. It does get easier and easier the more often you do it.

When it comes to creative pursuits, pushing through resistance is vital. Creative work doesn't have a set schedule or set hours from someone external, so it requires a discipline and an ability to overcome resistance in a much more obvious way than, say, getting out of bed and going to work or school. When you have no schedule, it's so easy to create obstacles and delays and excuses to delay getting to work. Some days when you push through, you're going to end up tossing out what you created. Other days you may find gold there. You won't know until you decide to take action. Resistance gets even more compelling when you're close to a real breakthrough. If you're nearing a real change in your life, or about to have success or finish something, your comfort zone and old brain patterns will sometimes push back with a vengeance. When you have the most resistance, when you craft the most outlandish, unbelievable excuses to avoid pushing through, these are the moments you need to muster everything you have to do it anyway.

Practice where it's easy. Practice on the MFR table, or with the little things like getting up to meditate instead of hitting the final snooze. Do that yoga pose even though it's hard. Do the dishes tonight, so you wake up to a clean kitchen. Sort and throw away your papers. Once you start to see that the things you are resisting aren't so bad, and they give you the results you want, it becomes more difficult to talk yourself out of them. Then when bigger, scarier barriers come along, you have developed your skills enough to move ahead more quickly in spite of them.

Why It Feels Hard to Push Through

Neuroplasticity is one of the most exciting new fields of study, as we are indeed upending our preconceived notions about what the brain can do. It also shows us why overcoming resistance can feel hard: because it is hard. From a biological perspective, we are literally wired to take the most efficient and energy preserving paths.

If our habit is to procrastinate, our instinctual brain wants to keep things status quo. It considers any new information as a threat, activating fear or anger to help defend the status quo. Neurologically, we are geared to resist the threat of change. This is why it's so hard to change habits.

What is required to override our habitual patterns is repeated focused attention. We have to practice. And practice. And practice. This is why meditation and yoga are such useful tools. This is why regular bodywork is so beneficial. The more often we practice doing something out of our comfort zone, and the more we practice discipline to push through our resistance, the more new neural pathways begin to connect.

As we discussed earlier, yoga speaks of our habitual patterns as *samskara*, which is literally described as "grooves" in our consciousness. Modern neuroscience shows that this is true: the more you practice thoughts and feelings, the stronger the pathways become. Much like if you were to pour water into an area with many grooves, the bulk of the water goes in the area where the groove is the deepest and most used. The ones that are more utilized are the ones that are stronger and more likely to be our default.

To get the new grooves or patterns more ingrained which will lead to the new pattern becoming our default, we must practice using it over and over, digging the groove deeper and deeper into our experience. Eventually, the new pattern becomes part of our habits. Like brushing our teeth in the morning, we start being able to do it without as much concentration.

One more suggestion is that it helps get the brain more on board with a new pattern if the reward systems and chemicals are activated in the brain when you do it. Some things (like exercise or meditation) naturally do that. When you form other habits, you may need to find a way to make it more fun or interesting in order to activate this system. If you are a person who loves the accomplishment of completing a challenge, then I suggest making a game out of whatever your new habit is. For thirty days, challenge yourself to do the thing that you resist, at least once a day. Then see if you can keep doing it or set a new challenge for yourself.

If you're taking on a big task, like breaking an addiction or replacing negative thoughts with positive ones when you've spent your whole life doing the opposite, you are going to need to be dedicated to your challenge for a longer time. Those old grooves are deep, so you'll likely need to push through several layers of resistance in order to establish the new ones. I highly recommend having extra and probably professional support as you undertake these bigger challenges, someone to give you hints and cheer you on.

If you don't have a specific area of resistance in mind, but you want to create a more positive experience for yourself, the best technique I can suggest is one that Erich Schiffman has suggested: meditate formally twice a day. Then for the rest of the day, take as many moments as you can to pause and come back to the present moment. Hear the sounds, see the sights, smell the smells, touch what is around you. Breathe. The more time spent in this connected space, the more your brain naturally rewires toward calm, peace, and happiness.

9

Freedom Compels Compassion
A Broader Perspective

I spent years undervaluing the gifts in my life and the divine order in how they appeared. If I hadn't experienced adversity and pain, I wouldn't be who I am or where I am. We bond over suffering. Our deepest, most authentic connections with people tend to involve compassion and empathy. We are amazing beings who can remind each other what it's like to feel love and, when someone is hurting, allow them to feel the connection that shared experience brings.

Because the focus is inward, and it requires a level of self-absorption, this process could easily be construed as self-serving. Self-awareness alone does not bring us to the state of happiness we all desire. These techniques will develop your ability to feel what is right and wrong for you. They offer pathways to peace and joy and lead you to embrace the parts of you that you have yet to fully accept. But true happiness will begin to reveal itself when the work you've done cascades upon your external life.

Once you are tuned in to your feelings, and following your intuition has become more natural, there is a level of freedom that occurs—the pleasant side effect of which can be increased spaciousness and joy, more of YOU instead of the tension that previously dominated. The miraculous part of this process is that when you allow your true nature to expand and breathe and pulse through your body, the impulses that drive you may start to shift.

It can be alluring to stay with the process of looking inward and feeling and processing your emotions because the contrast continues to give you the feedback of pleasure every time you expand or drop into your peace and joy. What can happen is that you become a sort of "processing addict," where your consciousness keeps giving you things to work with and problems to solve.

When I realized that my love for solving problems was continuing to give me more problems to solve, that was a day that woke me up to a new level. I was able to see more clearly that I could surrender to the joy that is cultivated in my navigation process, or I could simply decide that I've had enough fun solving problems and was ready for a new experience that flowed more with life. If my inner guidance constantly directs me toward the "more exciting" option, my life has more waves.

After you establish enough inner stability and sense of safety to relax and make space for more and more of your true nature, you will see that the love that is you is inclined to be of service—to yourself, others and the planet. This inner process rewards you with enhanced awareness of the loving divinity in every living thing. Automatically, respect and kindness increase. It becomes increasingly difficult to judge others, and compassion shines through. You'll be more aware of the suffering underneath bullying and violence because you've accepted these aspects in yourself.

For whatever reason, mentally ill or highly wounded people in the world are attracted to me. I have always felt uncomfortable when they approach me on the street and start talking to me. My natural instinct is fear and avoidance, so I tend to avert my eyes or say something to discourage interaction. Because I can feel the person's distressing sensations of being so off-center, those interactions quickly become unsettling. I had a recent experience with a mentally ill woman at the bank. I could feel myself withdraw and try to avoid the interaction that was about to occur. As she tried to get my attention and engage me, my mind began to judge her, deeming her crazy and weird and someone I should avoid. Part of this instinct is valid: Our inner selves know that if someone is unhinged, their actions might be erratic. But this scenario wasn't one where she was going to pull a glass bottle out of her cart and hit me with it. We were in the bank with people around. Though I still went into my pattern of avoidance, cutting short our conversation by expressing disinterest in the free keychain she was showing me, I *saw* myself doing it.

Immediately after the interaction, I recognized how I'd shut myself down and missed an opportunity to smile and be kind to this woman. It may have caused me a couple of extra minutes of discomfort, but it might have made this woman's day to be shown kindness in a world where she doesn't fit in and is likely suffering. Of course, I have no idea how aware she is of her own condition, but I could feel her pain, and a person in pain deserves compassion.

I was faced with a situation where instead of my heart responding, my tension reacted. I have learned not to judge myself for reacting, as the wounded part of me was showing up and needed compassion, too. Instead, I acknowledged what had occurred, and thanked myself for noticing. Then I spent a moment sending a blessing to the woman with whom I had missed my opportunity.

These are the golden moments in our lives. This is how it feels when more of you emerges. You can still do the things that your wounded or unconscious self has done in the past, but those reactions start to feel increasingly uncomfortable.

Luckily, because we are energetic beings, we can send out a mental apology and acknowledgment to the person we perhaps didn't act in our highest accordance toward. Or better yet, we can actually approach them and smile or apologize, if the circumstances are appropriate.

Our hearts know that we are all connected and that we are all divine. Our hearts know that the deep dark shadow aspects of ourselves are also divine. The mind does not see that divinity, and it loves to cast judgments, assessments, measurements, comparisons. That's what the brain is built to do.

As we free ourselves, we have no choice but to feel compelled to do the right thing. To paraphrase a teacher of mine, Ravi Ravindra, Christ didn't act lovingly out of his belief that he should act as such. He didn't have to *try*. He acted how he acted because it was his true nature. As we allow our minds and our bodies to soften, our hearts can lead the way. Compassion, kindness and service naturally pour forth.

Feeling Leads to Freedom

Nothing in nature moves in a straight line. Look at the rivers or tree branches. Look at how blood flows through your body, and how the airways in your lungs are fashioned. If nothing in nature moves in a straight line, why would we expect that our path would or should be straight? Expect twists and turns and rapid straightaways and pooling eddies. Embrace the beautiful dance of creation you are living in. Know that you can take as many walks off the path and into the meadow as you desire. And sometimes it's fun and exciting to trip and roll down a hill. Sometimes it's luxurious to rest and let your energy catch up to you.

The best part about this journey is that *you* get to create it. You get to decide to go left or right. Doing something that feels challenging or something that feels fun and easy is your choice. There's usefulness in all paths. But know that your miraculous, magnificent inner-navigation system is giving you signals all the time, and you get to choose whether to listen, how to listen, and what direction to take based on the information in front of you.

I vote that you do what you think is the most fun. If peace and calm are your game, enjoy that path. If adventure and excitement are what make you alive, follow those things. If you love solving problems, assuredly, you'll have plenty of opportunities to do that. Take your power into your own hands, and your own heart. Rest and relax in knowing that we all make it to the finish line. I humbly and lovingly ask that you learn to enjoy being here, in this very moment, as often as you can.

References, Recommended Reading and Resource List

For More About Fascia

Myofascial Release, Healing Ancient Wounds: The Renegade's Wisdom by John F. Barnes (MFR Treatment Centers & Seminars; 2nd edition, 2017)

Myofascial Stretching: A Guide to Self-Treatment by Jill Stedronsky and Brenda Pardy (Aardvark Global Publishing Co., 2006)

The Roll Model: A Step-by-Step Guide to Erase Pain, Improve Mobility, and Live Better in Your Body by Jill Miller (Victory Belt Publishing, 2014)

The MELT Method: A Breakthrough Self-Treatment System to Eliminate Chronic Pain, Erase the Signs of Aging, and Feel Fantastic in Just 10 Minutes a Day! by Sue Hitzmann (HarperOne; Reprint edition, 2016)

The Fourth Phase of Water: Beyond Solid, Liquid, and Vapor by Gerald H. Pollack (Ebner & Sons, 2013)

Gil Hedley videos for anatomy and fascial dissection (www.gilhedley.com)

For More About Trauma

Waking the Tiger: Healing Trauma by Peter Levine (North Atlantic Books, 1997)

The Body Keeps the Score: Brain, Mind, and Body in the Healing of Trauma by Bessel Van Der Kolk (Penguin Books; Reprint edition, 2015)

Choosing Gentleness: Opening Our Hearts to All the Ways We Feel and Are in Every Moment by Robyn L. Posin (Compassionate Ink, 2018)

For More About Yoga, Meditation, Mysticism

Yoga: The Spirit and Practice of Moving into Stillness by Erich Schiffmann, (Pocket Books, 1996)

The Wisdom of Patanjali's Yoga Sutras by Ravi Ravindra (or any of his books), (Morning Light Press, 2009)

Whatever Arises, Love That: A Love Revolution That Begins with You by Matt Kahn (Sounds True, 2016)

The Law of Attraction: The Basics of the Teachings of Abraham by Esther Hicks and Jerry Hicks (Hay House, 2006)

The Power of Now: A Guide to Spiritual Enlightenment by Eckhart Tolle, (New World Library, 2010)

Meditations from the Mat: Daily Reflections on the Path of Yoga by Rolf Gates and Katrina Kenison (Bantam USA, 2003)

Oneness: How to Live with Joyous Expansion, Ease and Lightness by Shalini Asha Bhaloo (Balboa Press, 2013)

The Four Agreements: A Practical Guide to Personal Freedom by Don Miguel Ruiz (Amber-Allen Publishing, 2011)

Anatomy of the Spirit: The Seven Stages of Power and Healing by Carolyn Myss (Three Rivers Press, 1996)

A Lamp in the Darkness: Illuminating the Path Through Difficult Times by Jack Kornfield (Sounds True, 2011)

All books by J. Krishnamurti

For More About Research and Science

Buddha's Brain: The Practical Neuroscience of Happiness, Love, and Wisdom by Rick Hanson (New Harbinger Publications, 2009)

Molecules of Emotion: The Science Behind Mind-Body Medicine by Candace Pert Ph.D. (Simon & Schuster, 1999)

Emotional Intelligence: Why It Can Matter More Than IQ by Daniel Coleman (Bantam Books, 2005)

The Power of Your Subconscious Mind by Joseph Murphy (Digireads.com Publishing, 2017)

The Biology of Belief: Unleashing The Power Of Consciousness, Matter and Miracles by Bruce H. Lipton (Authors Pub Corp, 2005)

The Keeler Migraine Method: A Groundbreaking, Individualized Treatment Program from the Renowned Headache Clinic by Robert Cowan, M.D. (Avery, 2008)

Suggested Bodywork and Healing Modalities To Explore

John F. Barnes' myofascial release

Craniosacral therapy

Reiki and other types of energy work

Meredith Sands-Keator's neural resonance work (geometryofhealing.com)

Eye movement desensitization and reprocessing (EMDR)

Peter Levine trauma release work (traumahealing.org)

Trauma Release Exercise (TRE) (traumaprevention.com)

Dynamic Neural Retraining System (DNRS) and other neural rewiring modalities

Holotropic Breathwork (holotropic.com)

Colleen Reid's BodhiBreath (bodhibreath.com)

Amyris Wilson Breath of Oneness transformational journey (amyriswilson.com)

Movement Therapies

Yoga

Somatic stretch

Qi Gong

Continuum

Other Rich Resources To Help You Dive Deeper

Erich Schiffmann audio files (Bigmindonline.com)

Kundalini Awakening Process (KAP)
(kundaliniawakeningprocess.com)

John F. Barnes healing seminar/live course (myofascialrelease.com)

Ravi Ravindra live events and audio recordings (ravindra.ca)

Yoga Anytime online courses (yogaanytime.com)

Matt Kahn and Esther Hicks on YouTube

TED talks

On Being With Krista Tippet podcast (onbeing.org)

Techniques

* Meditations marked with 🎧 will be available to download and listen to at LisaWestWellness.com/book-audio.

Acknowledgments

My path and my experiences are a culmination of the many great teachers and leaders that have come before me. I am forever humbled and grateful for the giants who have allowed me to stand on their shoulders.

The most obvious giants in my life are my teachers. John F. Barnes: Without your bold and unapologetic excavation of the internal landscape, realm of emotion and soul-body connection, without your brave stance and dedication to the emotional realm within the confines of the logic-centric world of medicine and science, many of the ideas that I have been exposed to and the tools to for living in that realm would not have been accessible. Also a special thanks to the amazing MFR therapists that I have met along this journey, especially Roxeanne, Cindy, Kathy, Tara, and Craig.

To my vast lineage of yoga teachers, most notably Erich Schiffmann, Kira Sloane, Ravi Ravindra, Patricia Sullivan and Linda Pon Owen. You have all taught me how to explore more deeply and feel more subtly. Erich, a special thank you for teaching me what meditation really is, for showing me the value of relaxation and for first exposing me to the advice: "Tune into the guidance and be brave enough to follow what you are being guided to do." And thank you for the invaluable online resources you provide to keep me tuned in and tuned up.

Thank you to Adam and Alana for your tenacity in coaxing me to delve into a disciplined practice of strength and steadiness, which prepared me to take a bigger leap than I thought possible.

To my Reiki master, Gladita, who first exposed me to the wonderful holistic world of energy, and to the many exceptional and powerful practitioners I have met throughout my journey, especially Eos Yolanda, Amyris Wilson, Julia Berkeley, Tiffany Carole, Meredith Sands-Keator, Logan Griffin, AnneDorthe Dryer and Virginia Lee for your loving and transformative healing techniques that have helped me to see and feel inside more clearly.

To Angie West, beautiful soul and editor extraordinaire, who gave me my first positive feedback and showed me how to clean up my work. To Michel Miller-Cicero, the sharp eye and wordsmith magician of an editor who cared deeply for the project and helped create a beautiful final product. This book would not be what it is without you.

Most of all, I bow humbly to the invaluable real-life experiences of the beings who are around me on a regular basis. Matt, your unwavering love and belief in me, as well as your mirroring and exposure to all of me (the good, the bad and the ugly) is immeasurable. To my mom and dad, and my siblings (the earliest, and still best friends in my life) and the people who made me into who I am. To all of my friends: You have made the hard parts more tolerable and life itself a hell of a lot more fun. A special thank you to all my soul sisters (you know who you are) but especially Amy, Winifred and Eos who know all of my deepest and darkest inner-secrets, my flaws and shortcomings and love me so much anyway.

Finally, but absolutely not least, I bow to my beautiful cats, Raymond and Mandy, who teach me daily how to be present, how to play, how to love, the importance of nature, and what loyalty, healthy boundaries and authentic expression actually look like.